Our Shattered Dreams

Martha Gutierrez

authorHOUSE®

AuthorHouse™
1663 Liberty Drive
Bloomington, IN 47403
www.authorhouse.com
Phone: 1 (800) 839-8640

Published by AuthorHouse 04/02/2016

ISBN: 978-1-4969-6320-8 (sc)
ISBN: 978-1-5246-0246-8 (hc)
ISBN: 978-1-4969-6640-7 (e)

Library of Congress Control Number: 2015901282

Print information available on the last page.

Any people depicted in stock imagery provided by Thinkstock are models, and such images are being used for illustrative purposes only. Certain stock imagery © Thinkstock.

This book is printed on acid-free paper.

This book is dedicated to my children, and to each and every man, and woman who is struggling in the process of becoming the best that one can be.

Because of you, I have learned to fly as high as I could to give you courage, and to show you that in spite of our shattered dreams, the sky has no limits...

Acknowledgments

This book came along as an assignment to me by God. The title, the cover, and of course, the context is an inspiration by the Holy Spirit. The glory and the honor are HIS alone.

Next, I want to thank my family for pushing me beyond my limit. Without them, I would not have been able to stop what I was doing in order to let the deepest of me be afloat and give birth to this book in your hands. There have been other people in my life for whom I have much gratitude, the ones who believed in me and always had me in their prayers, even when I was consumed with frustration and ready to give up.

Thank you!

I have tried numerous times to continue with this assignment given to me by God. But, of course, when something is a blessing, distractions and inconveniences block the way.

Where were we?

"Tell them," my mom says as she dries her hands on her apron. She is nearly done washing the dishes when she approaches the group of women around the table. They all look at me with expectancy and an affirmative gesture to start telling them… But, telling them what? I look at my mom questioning her with my eyes and the movement of my shoulders. She puts a hand on my daughter's shoulder as she leans on the chair in a comfortable position. She looks at all of the women there as if asking them to back her up to insist on my reply. In honor of my mother, whom I admire and love so much, I have no other choice but to share my shattered dreams:

"Who in the world does not have shattered dreams?" They all look at me with attention.

"Do you know of anyone who has nothing to say in this regard?"

There is silence… but then, all of a sudden Carmen says:

Chapter 1

Playing with Dolls

"When I was a little girl, my sister and I joyfully played with our corn-cobs covered with fabric scraps that we called "our dolls". We wrapped them with the odds and ends that we gathered from my mom's friend, the seamstress of the small town. I was happy and excited until cousins or friends came along and brought their real dolls. Can you call this a shattered dream? Not really, because I did not know any different. Guess what? My sister and I did have beautiful real dolls, but my mom did not allow us to play with them because she thought we might dirty them. What do you call that?"

As we are waiting for an answer, Dana starts talking:

Chapter 2

Christmas List

"I remember the Christmas Eves when the kids in my small town would be very excited to wake up the next morning to receive all the new toys and goodies from "El Nino Dios" – "Baby Jesus" or "Santa Claus" as a reward because they were well-behaved all year long. My New Year's resolution every year was to obey my elders and go the extra mile in every way to get that new dress or shoes on that anticipated Christmas Eve. That was my first shattered dream because I prayed every night for my wish list to be granted, but when the day came that I longed for so much, and I received something that was not requested, or sometimes nothing, it really broke my heart. I questioned my friends and cousins about what I was doing wrong. Because I saw that some of them were not behaving, nor were they obedient, yet they still received their wishes and much more... When I finally_came to know the truth about the gifts that "El Nino Dios" - "Baby Jesus" or "Santa Claus" supposedly brought to the well-behaved children, the shattered dream became a greater disappointment because my parents and my grandmothers knew how hard I had tried, yet they were not able to grant my petitions. I felt that they had all year long to grant the requests on my list."

Sophia continues:

Chapter 3

Small Town's Celebration

"You are right. We all have shattered dreams. I was invited to participate in a small town's celebration. My mom gave me permission. I was involved in the rehearsals, and I worked hard on getting everything ready. In the end, for one reason or another, I was not able to participate. Shattered dreams? Yes. I have cried many times in my life, and I think that as we grow older, the scars of our shattered dreams grow bigger and deeper. I am sure we all can relate…"

Margarita proceeds:

Chapter 4

Going to School

"I had my plans already set to attend high school, but my parents did not allow me to do so. Instead, I had to stay home and learn what I could on my own. Later I had to go to work with my mom. That was a big disappointment for me, because I wanted to be a certified professional accountant. I could imagine my diploma in that beautiful big frame on the wall behind my desk. Let me tell you, when I was daydreaming, I was the best CPA in the country, but that did not happen. Yes, I can definitely relate to the scars left by our shattered dreams."

I was eager to start sharing my experience in that area of the shattered dreams, but no way, I had to wait… Anna's voice was louder than mine, and she captured the attention of everyone present in the kitchen:

Chapter 5

Virginity

"I wanted to be a virgin when I married. I wanted to honor my parents and my husband with my character and reputation. I wanted my husband to walk straight and tall with his head held high, knowing that he was the first and only man who could call me his own. That was supposed to be my pride. I trusted everyone in my family circle. I was cautious about my friends and their families, but my own blood, my relatives? No way... To me, they were on my side, looking after my own best interest. At least, that is what I was taught by my mom and grandmas. Little did I know that my worst enemy was in my own home, living under the same roof with me..."

The eyes of all the women there were open wide, and our jaws dropped as Anna proceeded:

"It was probably two weeks before my 14th birthday, when someone very close to me raped me. That day, I died. Are these shattered dreams? No. No... For me, it was the end of every possible dream. After this, I went and I hid myself in a dark storage room to cry. I did not want to come out of there. I could not see anyone; I wanted to disappear from this planet earth. My mom was at work. My death happened in the morning; my mom was expected back home around 6:30 p.m., so I cried until there were no more tears to shed, and I was left dry inside. The person responsible for my death threatened me; if I told someone about what had happened, he would kill my entire family. I was scared, but I figured that my mom would notice that something was wrong with me. With the imagination of a child, I made a movie in my mind: I was going to come out of my hidden place with swollen eyes; my nose and my cheeks would be all red. Surely my mom was going to discover that something was out of line, and she was going to force me to tell her the truth... She would hold me tight and tell me that everything was going to be okay, that she would make this horrible person pay. Guess what? Even though I sat in front of her trying to get her attention, so she could see that I needed her, she did not notice anything, nor did she ask me if I was okay. It felt like someone had dug my grave deeper than 100 feet. Because, if my beloved mother could not notice my sorrow and help me, who would? I was overcome by darkness, and it felt like my heart stopped beating. You could tell that I was alive because I was still breathing, but I was killed that morning, and buried the evening of the same day."

At this point, we all stood up to hug Anna and show her our sincere compassion. But, she gestured to us to stay where we were. It seemed that she wanted us to listen to her pain as she was allowing it to surface for the first time, and it was screaming to get out. We understood and let her talk her heart out.

Ana was quiet for a minute or two so everyone could gain their composure again, and then she proceeded with the narration of her shattered dreams:

"Something interesting happened about a week or two before my death. I had my first meaningful dream. As you know, we have dreams here and there, but nothing that gets our attention. We tend to remember the most significant dreams. Well, this particular dream is still engraved in my mind and in my heart because it was like a warning to me. When I was in that dark storage room, I wished that I had said YES to the voice that I heard in my dream.

My dream is tri-dimensional.

6

First: I was a spectator. I saw the whole scene, myself standing by a river. I was the same age, turning 14. I was wearing a silky light pink full slip. I did not wear a bra yet. I was combing my long hair. Next to me there was a pale pink towel and a Dove soap of the same color. I walked towards the brook that was calmed and wide. I stepped into the clear light blue water. I could see all kinds of small and colorful fish as well as the different color pebbles and rocks under the water. The water was knee-deep.

Second: I am experiencing the dream. I bend forward, and my long hair floats on the water. I could see the oil separating from the water. I thought: "Oh my gosh! I did not know that my hair was this oily." All of a sudden, I felt a big hand. It was a huge hand that covered almost all of my head. I could feel the fingers on my forehead. I was calmed with no fear at all. As the hand pushed my head down into the water, I heard a man's voice asking: "Do you come with me, or do you stay in this world?" I did not answer. The hand pushed my head down deeper into the water. I could feel the water on my eyelids. I had my eyes closed, of course. The voice said: "For the second time. Do you come with me, or do you remain in the world?" As I said, I was at peace and calmed, but I did not answer. The hand pushed my head deeper into the water. This time the water was entering my nostrils. The voice said: "For the third and last time. Do you come with me, or do you stay in the world?" As I did not answer, the hand kept pushing my head deeper into the water. This time I could feel the water entering my nose and I started drowning. I replied and said: "I continue to remain in the world, I continue to remain in the world." The hand was immediately removed from my head. I lifted my head up. I could hear the drops of water falling on the stream. I looked around. I saw my light pink towel and my light pink soap. When I looked to the right, I saw the creek; hearing the sound of the water, I looked to the left, and saw the water coming fluidly and softly down the brook. Then, I looked in front of me. I saw the wide green field with corn plants. There was baby corn with corn hair of different colors. I also saw a house on the green hills. After that, my mother woke me up, but I could not move nor talk. It took a while for me to get back to myself, and be able to move and talk.

7

I did not share this dream with anyone. But, when I was in that dark storage room, I wished I had accepted the invitation to go with Him.

Shattered dreams? For me, all my dreams were broken. Nothing would be the same, or as dreamed anymore. Nothing!

I was still presenting myself as a normal 14-year-old girl, and no one noticed anything, but I felt like a living zombie. I hid my inner feelings. I was lost, buried, and forgotten.

Time went by as if nothing happened, I continued with the everyday living; morning, afternoon, and night. Every single day was an agony of counting the hours and the minutes to go back to sleep. I do not know if anyone that has not experienced this pain could even imagine. However, that was not the end, it was just a semicolon in my life. Later I found out that my body was changing, and my waist was not there anymore. Five months later, I started to faint when getting up in the morning. I began craving green apples with salt and lemon. I was experiencing shivering colds, and wanted to be covered from head to toe lying on the sofa. My mother started to question the whys. As for me, I blocked my mind. I pretended that nothing had happened to me. It was just a nightmare, a scary movie that I had watched. By now, my mother was concerned and took me to the doctor. Of course, the doctor started asking me about my boyfriend. What boyfriend? I did not even go out of the house. The next thing I knew I was going to have a baby. What? "By the Holy Spirit?" My mom asked. When we got home, my father almost killed me with his belt. As I said before, I was dead, so I did not feel anything. My family immediately started seeking the identity of the father of my child. They thought it was the neighbor's son, who was about 17, then my cousin, who was about 25. I did not say a word. The questioning continued, but guess what? When I finally told them, they did not believe me. Shattered dreams? Yes. Let us talk about that. I thought my mother would talk to me and explain what to expect, or what to do in this situation. In those days, the teachers at school did not get into those subjects, maybe in high school, but not in elementary school. I did not know anything, because I had never had my period. You guessed it. My mother never talked to me about anything related to my pregnancy. She never took me to see a doctor, nor did she give me vitamins. Nothing!

Shattered dreams? Let me tell you. My space was the four walls of that apartment. Sometimes the dead me wanted to resurrect and continue dreaming like nothing had ever happened, but I would kill her again and bury her deeper."

We were mesmerized by Anna's story. She took a sip of the now cold cup of coffee, dried her wet cheeks, and was getting ready to leave, but we all said in unison: "And the baby?" She got up from the table, went to the counter, poured more hot coffee into her cup, and continued:

"My daughter was born. When the time came, my father rushed me to my mom's gynecologist. He immediately arranged a bed in the hospital, and there was my daughter. I do not know if the doctor saw the reality of things, but he gave me something strong because I did not feel the labor pains. He just told me that when he said: "push" I was supposed to do that, and that is what I did. The doctor did not have any problem with me. I never saw my daughter. My parents decided that they were going to give her up for adoption. When I was taken to my mom's doctor, my father filled out the paper work, gave me a different name and he put himself as the father. I felt numb and wanted to die. I did not know what was what. Two or three months later, I had a dream in which I could hear my daughter crying. I told my parents my dream, and they brought my daughter to the house to stay. I was taking care of my little brother, who was three months older than my daughter. Now I was taking care of both of them. By this time, my parents moved three or four different times, hiding from the relatives and friends. They were trying to hide the sun with a finger tip."

We were all expectant to every word that was coming out of Anna's mouth. There was silence, no one moved. Finally, Anna said: "Enough of me. What about you, Susan? It is your turn to share your story with us."

Susan, who was sitting next to Anna, said:

"After hearing your story, I do not know if what I considered a dark chapter in my life is even worth telling." She got up like trying to gather her thoughts, brought a hot pot of fresh coffee to the table, served herself, and walking slowly holding the big cup of coffee with both hands, started:

Chapter 6

Masks In The Closet

"Imagine living a life of an estranged person in your own body. What? Yes. In front of people I was that perfect 15-year-old girl, with my parents, brothers and sisters, but I was pretending all the time. There were many different visages in my closet. At night, when the house was quiet and I could be me personally, I could not find me anymore. Somewhere in the masquerade I had lost myself. My life was a routine. There was no time to think. I did not want to be alone within my soul. There had to be noise, business, and the wearing of the masks.

It was time for me to wear a new mask. My parents arranged to have my identification altered, as I had to be at least 18 years old to get a job. That is what they did, and I went to work with my mom. The people at work were very kind to me; the manager always liked to have me work overtime. My first paycheck was greater than my mom's. I do not know what my mother saw, but she did not want me to work there anymore.

My parents finally realized that I at least needed to go to school to get a decent job, because someday I would need an income to fend for myself. So, it was time to wear a brand new mask. I wanted to achieve much when I graduated from high school. It was a very difficult time for my sister and me. She is three years younger than I, and had to play the same game, except that she did not seem to care about the outcome. We went to the same school, and we struggled with the classes. She just wanted to have fun, but I always had that competitive spirit. I had to learn and make it work. I do not know how I did it, but in the last two years I was in a good standing, and among those students who excelled in my class. The school sent the awards to my parents, but my mom did not pay attention, or those papers were not important to her, because I would find them in the garbage, or anywhere.

Finally, graduation time came. I was offered a job at a bank. I was very excited, as I basically had won that opportunity because of my effort and my excellent grades. My father decided that it was time for all of us to move. Shattered dreams? Yes. I had worked so hard on the presentation of my last work; the graduation was in a few days, but yes, you guessed it. I did not go. I did not even say goodbye to my teachers, and the job opportunity was given to someone else.

I was now 18. I once again picked up the pieces of another shattered dream to a certain extent. I had graduated from a business school, and I was excited to work in an office. I was a secretary with the ring on my finger to prove it. This time my father wanted me to work with my mom again; by then, she had found a job at a different company. I refused to do that. Why had I gone to school? One day we were driving by a bank, I saw the hiring sign at the door, and I asked my father to stop the car because I was going in to try. I did not believe in my ability to get the job. Well, I did. My daily routine was: go to work and come back home. My father sometimes took me to work and picked me up from work. Since I liked what I did, I dedicated myself to this task. I performed various duties there. After I had been working at the same company for three years, my boss offered to pay for my certification to become a loan officer. I accepted gladly because I wanted to learn. I was proud to tell my parents the good news, but my father immediately found fault with the occasion to advance. I ignored his comments, and the next day after work I went to school with the rest of the group who was taking the same class. I decided not to drive, and took the bus home after school that day. Waiting for me at the bus stop were my father and my brothers. My father was crazy mad. I was scared, and with a reason, because when we got home, he pulled the iron cord, and he started hitting me with that. I ran outside the house. I do not know how, or what happened; I was half naked, screaming, running down the street, and my father was running after me. The neighbors must have seen or heard me, but guess what? No one did anything, nor called the police. My father dragged me back into the house and continued beating me until he was tired and could not do it anymore. There was a time when I did not feel the whipping, nor could I hear his yelling. Everything started going black. I do not know if I passed out, or what… My mother was there, but she did not do anything. I remember my mother putting an ointment and alcohol on my back. My face was red and swollen; my forehead had a cut, and it was bleeding. The next day, my right eye was all red inside; it was impossible to go to work in that condition. I could not move. I called my job, and I had to wear a new mask again, to create an account of what happened to protect my father from going to jail. My will was broken, so my father dictated what I was supposed to say. The story was: when I was getting off the bus, two burly individuals, who wanted to steal my purse, attacked me.

I was not taken to the doctor, and of course, the police were not called. Three months had passed before I went back to work. Some of my co-workers thought that I was probably also raped. They assumed the worst because I took so long to return to work. Until this day, I have a scar on my forehead from the incident. Every time I look at myself in the mirror, I am reminded of those days and the dreams that faded with them."

By this time no one wanted to leave that kitchen. The hours passed, but it seemed like everyone there had to share the incident that had marked their lives at one point or another. The environment was safe and appropriate for each one of us to open up, and let the others know us better through our shattered dreams. Mary lifted up her hand requesting her turn to talk. Our eyes were set on her. She cleared her throat and started telling her story:

Chapter 7

My two lives

"I, like Anna, had a daughter at a young age, but my parents registered her, and raised her as their own. Time went by, and one day I met my husband. We got married. My parents decided that it was not appropriate for me to have my daughter with me. Anyway... I could not fight for her because my name was nowhere to be found on the birth certificate. Even though my daughter came to visit me once in a while, it was not the same.

My husband and I decided to move. We had saved enough for our journey and keep until we had found jobs. The typical starting family, a just-married couple. We ended up in San Francisco. It took us a while to get settled, and then our first son was born. Our little family-my husband, my son, and I were happy, and had so many plans. My husband helped me overcome all my fears and low self-esteem. He believed in me, and encouraged me to accomplish my dreams. We were young, and everything was possible. We saved our money. The amount assigned to our savings account was like any other responsibility.

My brother called me one day on his way to San Francisco. He had left my parents, and decided to live with my husband and me. He decided, he never asked us. Our lifestyle had to adjust because now we had someone with his own plans living with us. People with the same goals and dreams working together towards that accomplishment achieve peace and harmony in a household. It doesn't matter what the relationship of the third person under the same roof is, there is a change in the way members of the same team feel. My brother was living under my roof. Even though we lived together, his plans were different from ours. He complained about our way of living. We, not knowing any better, worried about his concerns, and of course, we tried to accommodate him the best we could. It should have been the other way around, because he was the one who came to us.

The next thing I knew, my brother felt that he was the owner, or the head of our home. One day my husband and I came from work, and found two other people in our apartment. They were relatives, and according to them, my brother agreed to them living with us. Can you imagine the different plans and ideals? I do not know if it was because we were young, or because we did not have the assertiveness to halt this situation. By then, my husband and I felt like we were the intruders. They were the decision-makers in a home for which we were paying.

After that, my parents came to visit. They brought my daughter with them. When I went to work, my mom would go through my drawers, and she found our savings passbook. She saw the balance of our account. She immediately shared the information with my father who did not take long to ask us for a loan. Of course, they were my parents, and I wanted to help them. But, the reason we left was because something similar was happening. Therefore, we did not want to have problems, and we denied the loan request to my parents. They were upset for a while, but they asked again. When we saw that the money we had in our account was the cause of different issues among our family members, we decided to invest it, so we bought a house.

We were buying our first home, and it was very exciting. The agent just took us to one property. Imagine living in a two-bedroom apartment on the second floor, and coming to this three-bedroom two-bath house, with a big back yard; we fell in love with the house. We wrote an offer, and it was immediately accepted. However, this was a short sale. It took approximately three months for us to move into the house. We were very excited and anxious to move. When we finally did, guess what? The house was dirty, and there were a number of things in which I thought the agent did not perform due diligence towards his clients, us, the buyers. That moving experience was a headache, but we stayed at that house for 15 years. We finished paying it off.

When our friends and relatives found out that we had bought a house, some of them were friendlier than before, and others stopped talking to us.

The time came when my daughter showed up in my life again.

No one knew I had a daughter. We had our house, the perfect family. We were very happy, and to everyone around us, we were the perfect family. One day I received a phone call from my mother telling me that she could not take care of my daughter anymore, and that I had to get her to come to live with me. At that time, I did not know what to do because my life was perfectly fine. I had given her up to my parents, and I was going to wait for her until she was 18 years old to make up her mind, and decide for herself what she wanted to do.

I had to digest the news and share it with my husband. He was happy and excited that we could have my daughter because he knew that every night and every morning we prayed together for her well-being. He was more convinced of bringing her to live with us than I. I was worried about my mom because I knew how much she loved my daughter. On the other hand, my daughter kept calling me every single day to tell me how many days, hours, minutes, and seconds we were away from being together again, and forever. I knew I could not fail her. I was concerned about how I was going to justify the fact that she was my daughter, I mean, legally. I had to register her at school, the doctor, etc. I could not sleep thinking about these things.

The time came when we went to pick up my daughter, the same day of her middle school graduation. When we arrived at my parents' house, she had all her clothes and her belongings in two garbage bags. She was ready to leave. In fact, that same evening after the ceremony, we left. Without a warning my life changed. From one day to the other, oops... I had to tell my close circle of friends and people in my life that I had a 14-year old daughter, and that she was living with me. Thank God everyone willingly gave their advice, and they showed genuine concern for me and my family, which now had a new member: my daughter. However, some of them wanted to know the whole story. How come I had this hidden daughter, she was 14, and hadn't I just celebrated my 6th wedding anniversary?

Shattered dreams? These have followed me everywhere. Now that I had a family of my own, the perfect family I had dreamed of, it was questionable. I have picked up the pieces many times. This time I had to confront the intrusive questions of my friends and acquaintances, and overcome whatever bleeding that the opening of the past lacerations might revive.

While the wounds were healing and the turmoil was settled, a new storm started. As my daughter was settling in her new home, with her 5-year-old brother, my husband and me; my parents and close relatives started visiting. I naively believed that each and every one of them was in my same court. Little did I know, they were poisoning my daughter's mind; I was the bad apple of the story. She began to grumble and rebel against me. I worked every day, but I did talk to her about those things. When she showed signs of improvement, we kept walking the road of life together anew. Another phone conversation with family, not living with us, caused us to regress to square one. We worked things out afresh, and continued with the journey of our new life together. It was a long process of going back and forth. The time came when she wanted to have a boyfriend. We had a long talk, and agreed upon on what she wanted. We gave our consent to have her boyfriend visit her at our house. He was not allowed to enter our home, but they could meet three times a week outside on the porch. By this time, my daughter was a couple of months away from her 18th birthday.

We were members of a church, and my daughter's boyfriend played the drums in the worship band. I thought that it was a safe environment and that we had our backs covered by the people attending service there. Within less than two months of my daughter dating this kid from church, the pastor of the congregation approached me. He expressed his desire to present my daughter and her boyfriend as a young dating couple, so they could set an example to the youth in the fellowship.

I consulted with my husband. He was not convinced with the idea, but in the end he agreed. The pastor said that he was going to come to our house to talk to my daughter and the boyfriend as to what the formalization of the relationship implied. We had not at any time been in a situation, or seen something like that, because we had never attended a church like this before; all of these protocols were new to us.

On the day the pastor and his wife were going to visit us, I cooked; I bought my daughter a new dress so it would be memorable to her. The pastor and his wife arrived, but they brought other two members of the church with them.

Shattered dreams? I do not know what else to call this experience:

We were all gathered in the living room. My husband and I were anxious to find out how we were going to proceed with this new task in my daughter's life. She was a teenager, a young lady who was excited to start a new stage in her life: dating. The first words the pastor said were shocking to us. My mind went blank. I looked at my husband, and his face was red. His features changed, and he stood up. The pastor continued as if everything was normal. He was requesting my daughter's hand in marriage to this young man who was her boyfriend. When my husband could finally talk, he tried to keep his good manners and express himself in a civilized manner, but that was not possible. He started to be polite, but his disappointment in the abuse of trust on the pastor's part overcame him. He lost restraint and told the visitors that if they did not leave our house immediately, he was going to start kicking them out, including the boyfriend. After they all had left, he continued the heated conversation with my daughter. He was convinced that she had known what was going to happen that night, and she intentionally had not told us. I believed my daughter when she said that all she knew was what the pastor had told us the last time we had attended church.

We stopped going to church. Days passed by, and I received a phone call from a lady attending that congregation. She told me that the pastor was planning a wedding for my daughter and her boyfriend in a couple of weeks from the day she had called me, because my daughter would be 18 years old by then, and that my husband and I would no longer have any say so in the matter; my daughter would be an adult, able to make her own decisions. This lady also told me that my daughter was in agreement with what was going on. I almost fainted. Of course, I had to confront my daughter. She denied it all. She was going to be attending university in three to four months, so I believed her.

As a mother, I sat down with my daughter and explained the birds and the bees. I told her that I would support whatever decision she made, but I wanted her to be honest with me. If it was because of someone else, in this case, the pastor's idea, I could press charges against him. My daughter kept telling me that she was going to school. After a few hours of long conversations, explanations of life and the meaning of marriage, she told the truth. She thought that she could get married and still continue going to school. The boyfriend agreed to that, and that was the real reason the pastor came to request her hand in marriage to this young man. Can you imagine how I felt? No. No, I don't think you can even begin to imagine it. I had to get out of her room, out of the house, and I went to the back yard to count to 1000. If I had not done that, I believe that indeed, we would have had a big family gathering, but for her funeral.

The pastor knew everything about my daughter, my husband and me. He knew our story. Why did he not tell us the truth? Why did he play Follow-the-Leader in a children's game? Now, my husband did not even want to hear the word "church" uttered in our home. Our journey together became bumpy, and the road was full of thorns. My daughter was on her way to university, so she would no longer be scratched. She was happy because she had her own agenda. Everything was fine until one day… I remember I was cooking dinner, when the phone rang. This time it was not a lady, but a man's voice on the other side of the line. He was an older man, I knew him. He was a much-respected man in that church. He told me that he knew that my husband and I tried our best to guide my daughter in God's way. He did not approve of what he had heard, and he wanted to warn us of the hidden plans the pastor, other older young men and my daughter's boyfriend were planning for that weekend. He really got 100% of my attention. He continued: They were planning to kidnap my daughter. He warned me to be careful, and maybe to call the police. I shared the information with my husband and my daughter. This time, my daughter's pale face and wide-open eyes told me that this was not in her plans. She was confused and scared. My husband called the police and passed the phone to me to describe the facts and to request protection for our daughter. However, the police said that they could not do anything, as nothing had happened yet, and that everything I told them was hearsay. They could not help me. I should call them only when something happened, and that they were busy attending real problems. I hung up the phone in disbelief of what I had just heard.

The clock was ticking, and the time was not going to stop. I had to do something. At that very moment, it was almost midnight; I called the elder men and women who attended that church. I expressed what was going on to each one of them. Some of them listened, and were willing to meet us at the church the next day to talk in person, some of them were concerned, but afraid to confront the pastor. Even though I had not attended that church for a few weeks, I showed up that day. There was only a small group present. I thanked them for being there. I explained the reason for my concern, and I requested their help to stop the plans of the evil men, including the pastor and my daughter's boyfriend. They all agreed to pray and cooperate with my cause. Five or six men got up and went to the pastor's office; they called him, and the men involved in the kidnap planning. Of course, they declined the invitation to join us at church, but they were warned of us knowing of their plan. We all were on the watch for their movements.

One evening, my daughter came running to my bedroom. She was scared and screaming. I thought she had seen a ghost or the devil himself. She could not even talk, she was just pointing to her window. My husband ran to the back yard with a baseball bat in his hand. Sure enough, there was a stack of bricks next to the fence. Someone had been watching my daughter from outside her window. We immediately thought it was her boyfriend, but then, what about the other men who were planning the kidnapping? We called the police. This time two officers came to our house. We showed them the evidence, and they wrote a report. We were all okay. They asked us to call them if anything bad happened. We had to wait for something bad to happen, in order for them to do something about it.

My husband removed the bricks, and due to the circumstances, he installed barbed wire on the fence to prevent any further access of intruders to our private property. We had to protect my daughter from whoever was invading her privacy through her window. Time went by, and the date came for my daughter to go to university. All of us were filled with excitement and hope as we accompanied her to the dorms. She was supposed to graduate in four years. She was anxious, excited, and happy to start her new journey. It was a new opportunity life was presenting to her for a better future. In the beginning, she came to spend the weekends with us at home. Later, she came to visit us one-weekend, and we went to visit her the following weekend. My daughter started to become more mature and better educated.

We spoke every day, especially at night; sometimes we would chat for hours. We would talk about everything, but she never mentioned that her boyfriend, the young man from church, was visiting her. I found this out through an older lady attending church. I asked my daughter, but she denied it. Yes. You guessed it right. The lady was telling the truth.

My daughter and I talked all the time. I believed everything she said, but she had her own private plans.

I started to notice that my daughter was more independent and distant. She no longer came to visit every other weekend, and when we were planning to visit her, she would tell us that she was going to be busy. Weeks became months. When I called her, she would not answer the phone. She started communicating with my parents, my sisters, and my brothers more. There were times when we went to visit her, but she would not be at her apartment. Everybody knew what was going on, except us, of course.

She was going to be 21. My husband and I planned a surprise party for her at the house. On Saturday, we would have a party for her friends, and on Sunday, the party would be for the relatives and our friends. We started preparing her birthday party for months. We changed the carpet, and we painted the house. Just a few days before the party, she came to visit us for the weekend. We were all excited and happy. As it

21

was closer to bedtime, she started getting ready to go out. She waited for us to go to bed to leave. As a mother, I never went to bed before I kissed each one of my children and prayed for them. The same applied to my daughter when she was home with us. When I entered her room to do that, she was preparing to leave. I told her that those hours were not appropriate for a decent young lady to go out. She ignored me and started going towards the entrance door. I rushed my steps and stood against the door to block her way out. "Why did you do that?" She asked. She was determined to go ahead with her plans at that hour of the night. I insisted that I was not going to let her do that. She grabbed me by my hair and started saying horrible words that left me in shock. I could not believe what was happening. She was beating me and telling me words that I never thought existed. She kept hitting me. I just could not get up, and because I was in shock, I did not defend myself. My husband was in the room with the kids, and he had the TV on in the other room, so he could not really hear what was going on in the living room. When my daughter did not stop mistreating me, I screamed for help, and asked for someone to call the police. When I said that, she stopped. She went to her room and started packing her things. Two officers arrived, but instead of stopping my daughter from leaving the house at that time, they told me that she was going to be 21, and she could do as she pleased. I did not have any right to stop her. She left. I felt devastated and in shock. The next day, the sunlight seemed sad and pale. I felt as if she had died, and we had a funeral in the family. This scar is the deepest I have experienced in my life so far.

Since everything was set for my daughter's surprise birthday party, and everyone we invited confirmed their attendance; I did not know what to do at that moment, for obvious reasons. My husband convinced me to talk to her. I called her, but she did not answer, so my husband insisted that we go to her apartment to see her. For the first time, I felt a stomachache, and nausea at the thought of going to look for my daughter. I thought that it should be the other way around, but we needed to know what was going to happen with her birthday party. We knocked at her door; she opened, and started talking to us as if nothing had ever happened. I felt hurt, and there was a whirlwind of unknown emotions inside of me. My husband explained to my daughter the reason for our visit. It was supposed to be a surprise party; we did not want to have the guests at the house without her, because it was to celebrate her birthday. She agreed to come. As I said, for her, everything was normal.

Before the unpleasant incident of a few days prior, I was always looking forward to visiting my daughter. I enjoyed the road to her place, but since the day that I was forced to go to let her know of our plans for her birthday, I hated the drive to that city. I did not want to go there, ever in my life again.

The day of the party came. I had not bought any present for my daughter. I have always given my children gifts with a meaning. This time I did not know what to get her. However, I did not think it was appropriate not to give her a present; she was turning 21, a very significant birthday. I gave her a pale pink, long dress. My husband got her a ring with her initial, and a bracelet. My feelings and emotions were numbed. I was like a zombie. I did not know what I felt inside of me, or if I felt anything at all. We both knew that we had a long pending conversation, but both of us avoided that moment, founding excuses to not be alone with each other.

My daughter's friends started arriving. They ate, had a good time with her, and my moment came.

I expressed my desire of wellbeing and happiness to my daughter. I told them that the instant she turned 21, my role as a mom had come to an end. I had done everything I could to make her a good, and responsible young lady; after that day, it was up to my daughter, and her decisions what she would achieve in her life. Her choices would determine who she would become one day in the future. If she was successful, or not, it was going to be up to her only. I, like Pontius Pilatus, washed my hands. I was no longer her guide, because she was going to do as she pleased anyway. My advise was not longer necessary. She had proved to me loud and clear what she was capable of. So, I decided to let her go. Everyone applauded. They stayed with my daughter until 11:00 p.m., or so, and left.

The Next day we were expecting the relatives and friends. At 4:00 p.m. every one started coming, but my daughter went to visit my sister since that morning, and had not arrived yet. Everyone was waiting for her. Finally, she arrived at the house almost at 6:00 p.m., but guess what? She did not even say hello. She took the cake and headed back towards the front door. I asked her what was going on. She replied that it was her birthday, and she had decided with whom she would spend the day. I could see through the kitchen window that one of my brothers and his wife were waiting for her in their car outside. I raised my voice and said: "No. No. No. I paid for the food and the cake. The party is here. Therefore, if you do not want to celebrate your birthday with us, leave the cake and go. I will take care of the situation here." She left. It was an embarrassing moment for me, but the guests stayed, ate, and we had a good time. My daughter did not come back home to sleep that night. I was not worried about her anymore. Now, my spirit was hurt, not due to my daughter this time, but because my brother and my sister backed her bad decisions. The only thing I could do was to pray for the best in the situation.

The next day, at around 5:00 p.m., I could see through the window that my brother in law was driving my sister's car, and parked on the street in front of the house. My daughter got off the car, and so did my sister. My daughter had a key to the house, so she opened the door, went to her room, and got all her belongings. My sister, who was waiting at the front door to get the things from my daughter, took them to the car, and put them in the trunk. They did this, back and forth, until they had taken everything. When my daughter closed the door of the house, and left without even saying goodbye, my whole world collapsed.

When she moved from her appartment, I did not know where she was anymore. My mother would call me once in a while to inform me about my daughter. I always pray for her, and bless her. She is my daughter, no matter what. Shattered dreams? You decide."

--Every time we gathered in my mom's kitchen, the group of women grew, and everyone brought something to make our moment together last longer while we ate, drank hot chocolate, or coffee, and enjoyed listening to each other's experiences in life. This time it was Helen's turn. She made herself comfortable and waited for every one to be attentive. Then, looking at each one of us, she said:

Chapter 8

Cancer

I turned 38. My youngest son was barely 5 years old. I started noticing that I felt very tired, especially after work. I had to lie down for 10 to 15 minutes before I cooked dinner. This happened every day. I could not understand why, because I was taking my vitamins. One evening, while I was taking a shower, I noticed that I had a small lump on my left breast. I did not know what it was. I was going to see my gynecologist the following week. So, I said to myself: "I will make sure not to forget to tell my doctor about this", and paid it no further attention.

The day of my appointment came. I went to my physician for an annual regular checkup. I forgot to mention the lump on my breast. We were catching up talking about the year we hadn't seen each other, different things while she was doing the routine auscultation; we were laughing about something we both said, but when she noticed the lump, her countenance changed to a serious, and worried expression. I asked her: "Is there something wrong?" She turned her back to me, and did not say a word. She made a phone call, then turned to me, and with the same serious expression on her face, she said: "I need you to go to the second floor. They are expecting you." I was worried now. "What is wrong?" I asked. "I need to make sure. Go, and when you come back, we will talk", she said. As I was walking up the stairs to the second floor with stray thoughts, I kept repeating myself: "She wants me to come back to her after I go to the appointment she made for me."

The appointment was for a biopsy. While I was there, they sent me to a different floor. They said that I needed to have a mammogram done first. I had never had this procedure done before. Everything that was going on was new to me. I had the mammogram done. It was so embarrassing to show my breast, and it was painful being pressed against that iron plate. The lady doing it apologized, but she had instructions to take it at a certain angle, and she had to press harder. I wanted to kick her and run away from that place. I thought that the pain was unbearable, but then it was over. After that, I went back to the second floor for the biopsy. I do not know which one was worse, the mammogram, or the biopsy. They inserted a big needle. I felt a painful burning sensation that made me want to scream, and my tears fell down my cheeks. But, finally this was also done. By this time, it was late. I went back to the doctor's office, but she was no longer there. She left a message for me with the assistant nurse. The message was that she would call me in a couple of days if there was something of concern, but if she did not call me, everything was fine, and there was nothing to be worried about.

The weekend came and passed. I did not hear from the doctor. So, I assumed that everything was normal, and that the lump on my breast was going to disappear with time. On Monday, it was raining. It was at the end of November. That day, on my way to work, I do not know what happened, but I lost control of the wheel, and my car was on the opposite side of the freeway. I managed to regain access to the right side of the road. I was so scared that I asked God to not let me die in a car accident like the one I had almost had that morning. Since it was raining, there was a lot of traffic; consequently I got to work late. Usually on Mondays the morning was a little bit stressful. My boss was answering the phones because I was not there yet. When I finally got there, I noticed that he was upset. He asked me why I was late and warned me that I should take care of my personal things, like appointments, etc., on my days off, or after work. He said that there was a doctor who had left five messages for me. He ordered me to return the phone call. While he was checking his mail, I called the physician. I was not thinking, in fact, I had forgotten about the ordeal of the week before when I went to see her for my regular checkup.

The receptionist answered the phone. When she heard my name, she did not even let me finish the sentence, but immediately transferred my call to the gynecologist, who said: "Helen, you have cancer, and I made an appointment for you at the same place where you had your mammogram done. They are expecting you. Hurry up. You must come right away", and she hung up the phone.

My grandmother had died of cancer in her uterus, but I thought that elderly people died because of different illnesses, including cancer. To be honest with you, I did not even have an idea of what cancer really meant.

My boss was still there by my desk checking his mail. He saw me hanging up the phone, and he asked me: "So, what did the doctor want?" I replied with a trembling voice: "She said that I have cancer, and that I have to go to the hospital right away." He kept reading his mail, and I do not know what happened to me, my mind was blocked. All of a sudden he screamed at me: "What?" He scared me. He continued in a loud voice: "Go. Didn't you hear that you have cancer, and you have to go now? Go! Go! Go!" When I was walking to my car, I felt if I was tripping into holes on the floor. I was so confused; I did not know what, or where, north, or south, east, or west. Looking back, the best way to describe it is like my spirit left my body, and I was walking by motion only; like a robot, without a spirit or soul. The traffic was so heavy, that it took me about two hours longer than usual to get there. During the time that I was alone in the car, I realized that I was going to die like my grandmother. I cried, not in desperation, but in resignation. I knew that there was nothing I could do under those circumstances. I made up my mind that I was going to tell neither my husband nor my children. I was going to make the necessary arrangements myself so when the moment of my departure came; everything was going to be ready. I would leave a letter to my husband with my wishes for my burial, etc. In those extra hours of driving from my place of work to the hospital, I was all set, so I thought.

When I arrived to the doctor's office, the receptionist looked at me with compassion, as if she knew that I was going to die. It did not bother me because I was calmed and surrendered.

The gynecologist took me in to her office. She explained to me that the different tests they did the week before revealed that I had cancer.

Therefore, she had made new appointments for me to determine what kind of cancer we had to deal with. She told me that she had requested a rush for the results, and that she would call me immediately to see her again.

I left her office, and as I was going towards the waiting room area, I saw my husband opening the door. He was wearing his yellow raincoat with the hood still on, all wet. I stood still. The expression on his face told me that he already knew that I had cancer. Unexpectedly, I broke into tears and ran to his arms. I thought in my mind that I was strong, but it was a lie. I felt so fragile, and I was afraid; I did not want to die. I had my husband and my kids, who needed me. After I cried and attained my inner peace one more time, my husband accompanied me to have those new tests done. After that, we quietly drove home; my husband just held my hand all the way to our house.

When we got to our place, I had several messages from my coworkers. They were concerned because I was by myself with such horrible news, they said. I did not have time to think of anything. My children got off from school; my husband and I picked them up. They were surprised and happy to see us because the babysitter normally did that. This time was like a party to them, so we took them out to eat and had a good time together. I did not know what to expect. Therefore, I decided to enjoy every second of my life with my family to the maximum.

The next day I went to work. Everyone hugged me and expressed their sympathy and good wishes. They kept telling me that I had to believe in the advanced science and technology, etc. That afternoon, I received a phone call from the nurse asking me to see the doctor the following morning. My husband and I went to meet with the oncologist. She tried to explain the best she could the situation at hand. She drew on napkins, and used different items, so we could understand the procedure, and what to expect. She kept saying that the cancer had not spread, that it was in situ. However, for some reason I knew in my heart that this was not the case. I felt it. We had planned our vacation in December. The doctor indicated that all our previous arrangements had to stop in order to take care of the most eminent thing at that moment, my life. The day before the procedure I had my final checkup. The physician was surprised that the lymph nodes under my armpit were also swollen.

The day of the surgery came, December the 8th. Even though I had everything ready and I was not rushing, inside of me I felt as if I was running as fast as I could because something was chasing me, and it was catching me. That day early in the morning, my husband took me to the hospital. I was given a hospital gown to wear. I was waiting for the nurse to call me. I was alone, and I retreated within myself. I felt scared; I had so many things pending and dreams unrealized. I was in the middle of an uncertain road. I did not know if I was going to see my children again. The nurse called my name to take me to the surgery room. I had never met the surgeon who would be performing the procedure. He told me that they knew where the tumor was, and they thought it was in situ, but it was not certain until he opened and saw what was really going on. He indicated that the oncologist had informed me that they were going to remove the lump. However, he was warning me that if he cut and discovered a different scenario, to not be surprised if I woke up from the surgery without my breast. I agreed. After that, they put the anesthesia mask on my face, and I was sedated. I woke up in the middle, or towards the end of the surgery. They put the anesthesia mask on my face again, and I did not wake up until I was in a recovery room. When I saw my husband by my bedside, I started crying because I felt as if I had been fighting in a strange territory, and I had just escaped from the enemy's camp; to see my husband was a relief. That part of the surgery was done, and I had my breast! Just a few hours later, after explaining to my husband and me how to take care of the wound, and setting up the next appointment, I was released from the hospital. My sister, the only one I have, and her three daughters, my nieces, were there at the waiting room with a bouquet of flowers. The look on my sister's face was of compassion and helplessness. They stayed with me for 10 to 15 minutes until we left the hospital. That was the only time my sister visited me even though we both lived in the same town. I went to visit her a few times because I wanted to feel her embrace and care.

I knew people from church, my children's school, their soccer teams, etc. Do you want to know how many people came to visit me or called me to find out if I was okay, or if I needed something? My kids' babysitter, a couple of friends, a pastor of the many I knew, and his wife, once. That was it. No more.

My daughter came once, but that was after I had finished my treatment. She did not come alone; she brought her boyfriend with her.

My treatment lasted eight months. Those eight months my husband did not go to work because he had to take care of our sons, the house, and me. I had to go to the doctor every two weeks, but I was always nauseated, in pain, and needing someone to force me to eat. God was always there. God was good to us, because, at my job, the owners helped me by my giving them my disability check, they would give me my full pay. That is how we made it through all those eight months.

When my treatment finished, I went to arrange my funeral, as I did not want last minute details. The lady there asked me to leave, because she said that I was crazy. She told me that my kids and my husband needed me, and that it was not my time to go, because I still had so many things to do.

I was scared because when I was on the chemotherapy and radiation, I believed that these treatments were controlling the cancer, but once those stopped, I did not know what to expect. I remember the last check-up immediately after finishing my last radiation, I asked the doctor: "Now, what else is to follow?" He replied: "Nothing. You will contact me if you find a lump in some part of your body, or if you feel sick." What I understood was that I was doomed to die, it was just a matter of reporting back to the doctor. I did not want to think about those things. Thank God I am still here!"

--We were captivated by Helen's story, when the phone rang. Even though no one answered it some took the opportunity to grab a glass of water or something, and immediately came back to their chairs to continue the journey with Helen. But, abruptly she said: "Of course, there are many shattered dreams in my life, but I also want to hear Elizabeth's story." We all looked at Elizabeth and waited for her reply. She put both hands on her head and started like combing her short hair with her fingers while she said: "Okay, let me think...." and then she continued:

Chapter 9

Change of Careers

"One of my brothers was in jail. He asked me to send him real estate books to study. I got the books he requested. Two or three weeks later, the books were returned. The books had to be sent directly from the publisher. Therefore, I kept the books, but one day, as I was cleaning the house, I threw them away. My husband saw them in the garbage can and picked them up. He encouraged me to read them and follow-up with them. I was not interested, because I did not want to be in a customer-facing position. I did not like sales. At least that is what I thought at that moment. Time went by, and I placed the books in a box to donate them to the Salvation Army. My husband retrieved them from the container, telling me the same thing.

One day I was invited to visit a church. There was a pastor who came from Ghana, Africa. I sat near the front. He was preaching, and he kept looking at me. At the end of the service, while people were eating, he approached me, and inquired: "Why are you afraid?" I replied: "I am not afraid." Then he asked me, "Why do you not want to study the books that your husband is asking you to read? There are many people who need you." He then left to converse with other people. I kept thinking about what he said, and I forced myself to start reading those books. I did pass the exam, and I became a realtor.

I was working for the same company for over 15 years. It was not easy for me to quit my job and start an uncertain career in which I would not know what would happen the next month, and so forth. I decided to do real estate part time after work. However, no brokerage would accept me as a part-timer. So, I determined to start my new career as a realtor until my boss fired me. One day I received a phone call from the broker of a new company; he would not have any problem accepting me to work part time in this new career, as a real estate agent. I went to his office, and from that day on, I kept going every day after work. I had to get a cell phone, and he ordered me business cards. I started giving my cards to whomever I encountered on my way.

However, to my surprise, the people with whom I spent more time during the day than with my own family hurt me; somehow a business card came across their path, and my boss was furious. How in the world was I planning to venture in this challenging and uncertain career? Was I crazy, or what? She asked. I was trying to articulate my reply, when she continued with her questioning, which sounded more like harassment: "Didn't I know that the real estate agents have those nice cars, not that raggedy dirty car? Real estate agents dressed posh, not like an old town teacher." I felt humiliated. She was upset, or I do not know what, but she let me know how she really perceived me in her heart. She did not even let me express myself, and left. The next morning when I got to work, I found my replacement sitting on that chair, at that desk, where I had sat for over 15 years. I was confused, but I finally said: "Hello." I was completely ignored. Then, the people who had worked with me for all those years came in, and they acted like I was not there. To them, I was invisible. I did not know what to do, so I took the keys to the office from my purse, put them on the front desk, and exited the building. I went to my car and could not stop crying. I went to a park that was near the office to cry out my disappointment, and when everything came out, I called my new boss, the broker at the Real Estate Office. I explained to him what had just happened to me. He was so excited, and he gave me all the encouragement that I did not get from the people I had just left. I stopped by my new office. I was assigned a desk, and everything was ready for me to start my new journey as an independent contractor, a realtor. The broker, and all the realtors there made me feel at home. It did not take long for me to adjust to this new way of independently working. To my surprise, I liked it. My husband and my children supported me in my new adventure.

When I was studying to become a realtor, people at church, my friends, and relatives promised to wait until I passed my real estate exam to buy or sell their homes with me. Well, now that I was 100% ready, I called each one of them, mailed them, or personally gave them my business cards. They all promised to work with me, but guess what? They purchased, or sold their properties with someone else. It was a heartbreaking experience, but life had to continue, and I had to find the way to make things happen. I went to the mall, and I started talking to people. That is how I got names and phone numbers of possible clients. After a while, I was so busy that I did not have time to look back and regret any of the things that I had recently experienced from my friends, relatives, and ex-coworkers. However, the people who have known me for years, my friends, and relatives stopped calling me or visiting me. There were times when I felt sad and lonely. I did not understand this change. I visited them; they looked and sounded happy and excited for me, but their actions showed me the real intentions of their hearts. God blessed me with new people, clients whom I later adopted as friends. I had a big circle of friends. I helped so many people that I did not have time to think of all those disappointments of the previous months. The first year I made eight times more than what I made at my former job. I was very excited. Later, my family started to get closer to me, and I was able to assist them when they asked me for help.

My sister called me one day because she was looking for a job. I happened to know that the mortgage broker with whom I was doing business needed an assistant. So, I told my sister, and she went to see him. Of course, she got the job. She was basically helping him with all the clients I sent him. Then one day, she did not have a job with him anymore, I recommended my sister at the office I was working for. My broker indicated that I was very busy, and that I should have a personal secretary. What a better assistant than my own sister? She started helping me. I gave her a salary.

On one occasion, I went on vacation with my family. I left my sister in charge of my transactions. When I came back, my sister surprised me with the news that she had passed her real estate exam, and now she was also a realtor. She had done all her studies in secret. I thought that was not nice because she was working with me, and not to share this accomplishment? I did not want to think badly, but that action made me wonder. Later I found out that some clients purchased their house with her. I did not pay too much attention to that, because they have the last say. My sister called me one day to let me know that the people to whom she had given my business cards when she was working with me were her clients now. So, I erased their names from my database. I respected her wish, but it distressed me to know that she was contacting my clients. Why? Days later, my sister left the company and joined the competition. We kept being family, but my dreams were shattered in regards to the plans I had with her.

I became a real estate broker; I owned an office building, and I opened my own company. I was planning to have a beauty salon, a mortgage company, and some other businesses related to the trade. I shared my idea with my sister-in-law, who was working for a salon. I encouraged her to get her license and start her business in one of the offices at my building. She agreed. My sister and I helped her with the finances, but in the end, she kept the funds and opened her business somewhere else. After that, I offered the opportunity to the lady who cut my hair for years before I went to my sister-in-law. She accepted and opened her second beauty salon at my building.

I had this loan officer. We had several transactions together, and we became friends. We took our relationship to the personal and family level. When I took possesion of the building, I asked her to rent an office from me so we could work more closely. She was very excited. My husband started fixing the building. Once in a while she passed by to see how the work was going. She liked to talk to my husband. I did not notice anything wrong. However, I do not know if it was real or an illusion, but people started planting seeds of mistrust regarding her. I started to notice things that I did not appreciate coming from her, because I really trusted her. It came to the point that I had to confront her because she made some situations very obvious. I do not know if she did it purposely to make me doubt my husband, but she did not stop her flirting with him. It seemed like she did not care what I felt, and she kept pursuing her goal; it was like she was daring me. I stopped working with her, and of course, I had to find a different mortgage broker for her office. Luckily, I found someone, and the person who moved in was very nice. I organized breakfasts, lunches, or dinners for my clients. We categorized people into groups and invited those whose house anniversary was coming up in the same month, and two months ahead. The purpose of the invitation was to find out if they were going to sell, buy another house, refinance, or just keep their house. I invited different speakers, title companies, different lenders, etc. I gave priority to the tenants who were renting from me.

Later, I found out that the mortgage broker was passing my clients to her husband, who was also a realtor. When the one-year lease was over, the mortgage broker did not renew it. That unit was vacant all the time. Later, all of a sudden, the ceiling collapsed. It seemed like that office had a curse upon it. Everything failed.

All the tenants, one by one, left. The office used as a beauty salon, was the only one occupied, but with a different tenant, and mine of course. The whole building looked like a ghost. It was a desolate place. Sometimes I would find homeless people sleeping in the hallway. The stairs smelled bad because of the people who spent the night under them. They would relieve themselves anywhere. Can you imagine the scenario? It came to a point where I also left. It took me time to digest the idea of leaving, but one morning I woke up, and got the conviction of doing it. So, I moved and never returned.

Behind this building investment, there is a story. Would you like to hear it?"

Of course! Everyone in the kitchen screamed. Elizabeth stretched a little, and continued:

"Well. My husband is the one who made the deal with the sellers who were also realtors. They had been occupying my office before. The idea did not excite me. In fact, every time my husband brought this subject to our conversation, I got stomachaches, or diarrhea; and sometimes both. I did not know why, but I avoided talking about that, nevertheless, we had to do it. He was so persistent with this idea that we finally made the purchase. To make a long story short, I felt like I was forced into the project. The interesting thing is that all the units in the building were vacant, except for the owners', who used the office that later became mine. I did not pay attention to that, because the building needed new painting and some repairs. Since we were going to renovate the building, it did not matter that it was vacant. After the tenants left, it looked almost like the same way when we bought it, except that now it had color, but it was vacant and desolate. However, the concept that I wanted to share with you is the following:

Years before, I would say three or four years before the purchase of this building, I had this dream:

It was the same building; I went up the stairs with many people following me. I was taking some people to my office. I knocked at the door, and a person opened it. It must have been a woman because her toenails caught my attention. They were pink fuchsia. I could not see the face of that woman in my dream. Then, I went around my office through the hallway and got to the office where the mortgage broker was. There were so many people following me that they were standing in the hallway. I started bringing all these people at about 3:00 p.m. When they were standing in the hallway, it was already late, around 7:00 p.m. It was dark. I needed to use the rest room, and since there were so many people I could not use the ladies' room there. So, I went to the parking lot parallel to the building, facing the corridor. Because it was dark, I went behind the bushes on the corner of the parking lot. I had my underwear down, and I was in the squat position to urinate. All of a sudden, somebody turned the lights on, and I was exposed. Everyone in the hallway was pointing their finger at me and laughing. I did not know what to do. I was very embarrassed. Instantly, Jesus, wearing a long, flowing white dress, stood in front of me facing the people, and extended his gown to cover me. I did get up and pull my underwear up. I was so thankful for the intervention that my heart trembled in gratefulness to Jesus. I leaned my body and put my hands and arms on Jesus' back. Everyone there was quiet when Jesus appeared. He stopped them from ridiculing me. Then I woke up.

All these years had passed by, and I had forgotten about that dream. But, one day I was coming from lunch. I was waking on the street beside the parking lot. All of a sudden, the dream came to my remembrance. I had to stop and look at everything that my physical eyes were seeing, because it was exactly the way I had dreamed that building. I felt the chills all over my body, and I was speechless. I knew that I had to be cautious. The interesting thing is that the mortgage broker took advantage of the people who trusted me. This person used my reputation with the clients, to recruit them with the backup that she was working at my building. Everyone thought that I was endorsing her wrong doings. Of course, I did not know what she was doing. All I knew is that many people passed by my side window towards her office. Sometimes, I saw clients passing by to her office, and I thought they were going to stop by to say hello, but they did not. I tried to make all kinds of excuses, but the reality was very different. The mortgage broker was bad mouthing me with the clients. The sad part is that they believed her. So, my clients and their families, who knows what they thought, but I could see the difference in the way they behaved towards me.

Shattered dreams? The lady, who was renting an office for her beauty salon, was sending the clients to her friend realtor. I felt that everybody in that town knew what was going on in my life, so I started receiving fewer phone calls from new clients. I was working twice as hard to try to help people modify their loans, but I was doing it for free. Little by little I did not know what to do. I had to force myself to go to the office. I felt tired and sad in that place. I did not realize how much I had waited and tried to hold on in that building. The day I did not have to come back there, I felt relieved.

I, like everyone else, have many shattered dreams, but for the sake of time, and in consideration to the rest of us here, I pass the privilege to Doris."

--Doris was washing the dishes. While we were waiting for her to come to the table, some made phone calls, some checked their messages, and some stayed still anxiously waiting to hear Doris' story.

"Where do I start?" She said. "I know. This is what comes to mind" she paused and then proceeded:

Chapter 10

My Down Fall

"I was working from home. I started to gain weight. Since I did not have distractions, I was able to pay more attention to what was going on in my house. It is sad to say, but I noticed that my husband and my kids expected the house to be clean, the food to be ready and for me to produce much more in my work from home. I did not pay too much attention to these details in the beginning, but every day the tone of voice that they used when the house was not clean, or the food was not prepared, made me realize that they did not have consideration for me at all. That hurt. I expressed how I felt, but they kept their same reaction when some things were not done. I became more a housewife than a sales person. They did not care if I had appointments during the day or not, they would just take the cars. If I told them the day before that I was going to need a car, sometimes they would respect that and not take the car, but other times, they did not care. There was no consistency. Every day or every time doing the same thing; the scenario changed. I felt that neither my plans nor I were important to them. I was living in the same house with them, but at the same time, I was alone. I was just the maid.

When we moved to live at that house, we rented storage to store the majority of the furniture. Imagine; we had furniture for a 4,300 sq. ft. five bedroom, three bathrooms home, and to move all that to a 2,100 sq. ft. four bedroom, 2 ½ baths, was just impossible. We had to rent storage. However, when we moved to this smaller house, we did not use the services of a moving company, we did it ourselves. So, the things were left everywhere and anywhere. We all got tired. Day after day, the things remained in the same place where they had been left on day one. I tried to make this house feel like my home, but the day was not enough to do everything and fix the things as I would want. We always had company, my sons' friends. I was embarrassed that the house remained like we had just moved in, when months and months had already passed. There were heavy things that I could not move by myself. When my husband and my sons were home, I asked them to help me, but instead, they complained or agreed to do it, but they never did. Months became years, and the things remained in the same place. Well, moved a little bit, but that house was like a hotel, where you just go to sleep. I felt down or sad most of the time, because I was the only one who stayed home every single day. I had my personalized schedule as to when to do laundry, when to clean the house, etc. I just saw my husband in the evening. Sometimes he had already eaten out and just came to take a shower and to go to bed. Our dinners together as a family started to disappear. Everyone did as they pleased and had their own and separate plans. I cooked, but sometimes I was the only one eating my food. But then, guess what? I decided not to cook for anyone else except myself. Then they would get upset at me because they questioned what I did all day long at home.

Shattered dreams? I did not feel appreciated, but rejected. I opted for staying in my room and did not get out for long periods of time. I got out of my room only when they called me for something. Sometimes, I stayed there all day long until the evening. It came a point in my life that I did not feel like taking a shower or changing my clothes. I felt more comfortable at home than anywhere else. I did not know it yet, but it was a problem for me when I had to keep an appointment. I started making excuses. Sometimes I postponed or canceled the appointment. I did not realize it, but I started being forgotten in the midst of all the disappointments and not understanding what was going on with my life. I called different people, trying to find an answer to stop my desperation. But of course, everybody was busy and they themselves were in predicaments; How could they help, if they had many and different needs? Some people thought that they knew it all and started telling me to read this and that self-motivational books. Some said that it might be a punishment from God or a lesson to be learned. I did not feel helped at all. By me talking and talking to others, I heard myself and found the relief one way or the other. One thing is for sure; I did not have goals or dreams anymore. I felt like I was dying from the inside. I felt weak and tired of life itself. I was caught up in a vicious cycle causing depression. I was getting up every day, and instead of seeing an opportunity to do something fruitful for the day, it felt like waking and getting up was an agony. I was forcing myself to do something and find ways to find myself.

Shattered dreams? Almost four years in that house, and the boxes did not move. My resolution for 2013 was to clean the house. I asked my husband and my sons to help me move the heavy boxes and furniture. They did, so I cleaned the house. It took me two days to accomplish my goal. At the end of the last day, I felt so tired that I felt my feet tingling, and my whole body ached. I tried to maintain the cleanliness of the house. As I mentioned before, my husband and sons tried in their own way. But in order for me to keep the house clean, I had to go after them, picking up they left overs, or whatever they left anywhere.

Since I had all the time at home, I started analyzing, trying to find where we started going down. I wanted to find out where everything went wrong so I could correct it. There were so many different things, but the main one was that I was disobedient to my God "feeling". The Holy Spirit always guided me. Sometimes I strongly felt not to do certain things, but because my husband thought differently, I obeyed what he said. Sometimes it was the opposite of what I felt or he stopped me from the original project assigned to me in that particular moment. Therefore, I saw myself in turmoil or situations that I could have avoided if I had just been obedient and done as instructed by God.

Everything has a reason for being. Our struggles have a purpose. Therefore, I do not complain anymore, but when I was going through them, I complained and questioned others and myself for the different situations. However, now that the wounds do not hurt as much, I am able to distinguish and see. God has been merciful. In a way He warned me through dreams of the messy rivers that I was going to cross, so when I did I would not be surprised and be ready to do it, knowing that He was with me all the way. He allowed the situation or circumstance to arise, so I could learn after going through the water or the fire, to overcome it. He wanted me to be stronger than before to be able to help others who were following me, because one day they would have to cross the same rivers or similar ones in life.

Before my downfall, I was very active and had everything under control at home, financially and the complete household management, including the kids' studies and all. We all had a peaceful and tranquil life. We had our vacation every year; our bank account was cushioned, and we were all happy and excited. The daily challenges and trials were small and simple to handle. One thing is for sure; I was very passionate and revolutionary. I fought for what I thought was right.

Looking back, when I was so active with the kids, the house, my work, etc. I longed for one day for myself. Now that I had to rest, I longed for those active days. I am telling you. It does not matter what situation we are in, we always long for something else, or for what we once had and did not properly appreciate.

Now, I believe everything my loved ones, my husband, and my kids tell me. A new kind of me emerged after the forced rest I had to take. To be honest with you, I like this new Doris, calmed, relaxed and peaceful. I have had many shattered dreams, and I am sure I will have more in my life time, but from each one of them, I am learning and becoming a better human being."

--This time we all applauded Doris, as this was the last story for the day. But, before we left the kitchen, Heather was nominated to be the first one to share her experiences at our next gathering together.

As usual, we were eager to learn from each other's lessons in life. Heather was nervous, but Angela made sure that everything was in place to make Heather comfortable and ready. Then, suddenly, Heather said:

41

Chapter 11

My sons

"I believed and trusted everything I was told. I always believed that the people living under the same roof constituted a family, and all members were in the same team pushing forward towards the same goal. Once a member of that family decides to start a new family of his or her own, then the interest of that family member is separate from the rest of the team still remaining in the same household, under the same roof. That was the case with one of my sons, who decided to start his family at an early age. But of course, he came to visit us often. Sometimes he took milk, cereal, or whatever he needed to his new place. That, of course, slowed us all down, because that family member was not supposed to take from us. It is not right or fair, but the example was set for the others to follow.

When my other son had his girlfriend, he started doing the same thing; using our car because the tank was full of gas, or because it was clean. See, every dollar that he could save at our expense, he thought it was wise on his part. Later down the road, he started bringing his girlfriend to our house. Of course, the girl just sat down, and I had to entertain her. I understood that the first, second and third time she felt uncomfortable, not knowing us, but after that the same thing continued. No. It is not right. The point is that my son and his girlfriend were caring for their interest, but they were using our funds and efforts to save their own to use it somewhere else. By allowing this, our process of advancement was slowed even more now. Two sons taking our blessings, it was impossible not to notice the shortage. The third son started dating. Again, a dollar or two that he could save to take his girlfriend to the movies was good, but at my husband's and my expense. By this time we had three sons having their own separate interests, but taking from our effort and our blessing. One was not living under the same roof, but as I mentioned, coming once every weekend or every other weekend to take from us, we could feel it financially. The other two were under our same roof, and doing the same thing every single day, the load became heavier and unbearable. In the past, families thought that the children were a blessing because they helped the parents. I know that my husband and I did help our parents until the day we got married and left our respective families to start our own. Even so, once in a while we financially helped our parents. In my case, with my children, it was completely the opposite; instead of helping, they were taking away from me. It came to a point when we could not pay the rent; the main services were interrupted, and the funds were not enough to cover all the responsibilities every month. In the meantime, my sons were saving their money, and my husband and I were short every month.

Every day that passed, I realized that my husband and I were alone again as we started. I cooked for all of us, my family, living under the same roof. Each one of my sons went to eat out with their girlfriends, and did not care for my food anymore. I used to wait for them to close the door and go to sleep at peace, knowing that everybody was home. One started coming back home at 11:00 p.m. the other one at 11:45 p.m. Sometimes their return home was later and later, to the point that I fell asleep waiting for them. When I woke up I went to their rooms to make sure that they made it back home, then I went back to sleep. This routine was almost every day, as it was rare the time when they stayed home. They also started not picking up after themselves. I felt like I was their maid instead of their mother because there was no consideration to my efforts at all. That is when my husband and I decided to talk to them. We told them that if they did not help in the house, we were going to terminate our lease there, give the keys back to the landlord and leave. They did not want us to do that; they agreed to help even financially to ease our burden. My husband and I were happy, because our sons told us that we were needed in their lives. But, guess what? Those were just words. When the time came to pay the rent, they failed to come up to their promise. That same thing happened, once, twice, three times. By this time, we could not come up with the rent money, so we left the house. We did not have any other choice. I always believed what my kids told me. But, of course, I had bad experiences every time. I forgot that I should have known better, because I was the mom, years older, and more experienced.

Shattered dreams? The wounds that have left me with deep and big scars are the ones that were caused and created by my own sons. You go figure. I presented my children to God. I always brought them to church, read the Bible with them, prayed for them every single night and morning. What happened? I always believed that families who prayed together would never be separated. Then, what went wrong? I always treated my children with respect and took care of them the best I could. I have believed that I have been their babysitter, and that they are not mine, but God's. He provided my husband and me with health and financial means to take care of them and guide them through life in a Godly way, to equip them to have a family of their own one day. I envisioned for them to graduate from university, get married and have a family. Everything started with my oldest. He graduated from high school. He decided that he was going to take six months to go to college or straight to university. He got involved with his girlfriend. He thought that he was already a man, but living at his parents' expense. He started early in life to have the responsibility of a household of his own, but he was not properly equipped. He thought that he knew better than his parents. And, yes. It is our fault. As his parents we were supposed to let him experience the responsibility that he thought he could handle on his own. He needed to know that he could not come to his parents' house for food or money. I am thinking that if that had been the case, he would have experienced the reality of life and had decided to go to school and wait on the big man's responsibility. I think my husband and I were too compliant, and instead of helping him, we actually harmed him. Yes, I agree and accept that he took different courses and passed different licenses. However, he is not satisfied, he is not happy. I know that he regrets not having continued his studies until he graduated from university. He wanted to be a heart surgeon. When he found out that he could not tolerate the sight of blood, he realized that he was not going to be good in that field. Then he wanted to be an attorney, but as you know, he settled for less than what he was capable of. Everything has been very easy for him, because his parents have always provided, even though he does not recognize that. He covers his dissatisfaction by blaming his parents for using money unwisely and not thinking about his education. Why? Because now that he has tried to enroll himself to go back to school, he has to pay, and since he has to work, it is hard for him to accomplish both. Well, what can I say? In the beginning, I tried to offer him different ideas to make his plans easier to accomplish. Then I realized one very important thing: When the parties of a household are not going and working together towards the same goal, the plan or goal is distorted and burdensome to the guide who believes that the strength and efforts of all the members are directed to the same target, but they are not. That is exactly what happened in my son's case. My husband and I went the extra mile for him. He made us believe that he was of the same mind with us, but in reality, he was just using us to accomplish his short-term plans. What hurts the most was the fact that it was not for his pleasure or satisfaction, but for his friends' as well. I want to believe that he did not know the effort and sacrifice we had to make to assist him every time he asked for our help. The first time, we happily did it, the second time, the same, but the third and fourth, it became burdensome and fatiguing. I have to be honest with you, every time we saw his number on our caller ID, we hesitated to answer the phone, because we already knew that he was going to be asking for something. Sure enough, the car broke down; the rent was overdue, etc. Even though we expressed our dissatisfaction or gave him a lesson for the 100th time, we ended up helping him anyway. I figured that he knew the tactic and did not care how we felt, but all he cared about was getting what he wanted at the moment. Since he was living by himself and not under the same roof with us, we did not know exactly what was going on. We believed the stories that he made up in order to get the funds or means he was requesting. I do not know how to explain it, but he became so inconsiderate towards his parents that his actions felt in the selfish and self-centered category. The reason for this conclusion is because he pushed us to the limits where he did not give us any other option but to help him. Why? Because I figured that he knew that we would do anything not to see him involved with the police or doing something illicit. For instance, I did not have any money. I had to borrow because he made the situation sound so extreme that it was life or death. I felt pressed against a wall, and for the first time I noticed the true colors of the son - parent relationship. It was sad to realize that my son did not care how much of a struggle he put us through; all he knew to do was to ask. What can I say, he asked, he demanded money to cover his deficits because he did not care to budget. He cared less if we died with the intent to accommodate him. I tested him on different occasions; it hurts to accept that he failed every test I put him through. I did not want to wake up from the dream I had made in my mind about my son caring for me and his father. No matter how much I wished that he would consider us and work towards the same goal, which was to cover each other's back and keep stepping up to accomplish each one's goals, that was not the truth. In the meantime, I was already behind in paying money back to the people from whom I had borrowed it in order to help my son keep up with his financial responsibilities. One day, while I even had a headache from the stress of figuring out how I was going to make it towards the end of the month to cover the main necessity bills, I made up my mind and promised myself to never borrow again. When my answer was in the negative to my son's requests and petitions for the same thing every time, he started blaming me for his lack of funds. I was to blame for him not being able to graduate from university, for his small pay checks, etc. I tried to explain and give him the reasons for his current experience, but there was no way that he would let me talk. My spirit became so frightened listening to him shout that I decided to be quiet and just let him say whatever he wanted to say. It did not matter how I tried to say something; I was not allowed because his tone of voice was so loud and his words, like a river, did not stop so I could defend myself. I gave up and started experiencing something that was strange to me and never thought that I would feel towards my son. Indifference. Could that be the appropriate word? I developed this feeling of not caring or giving up on the cause I had fought for all my life, which was not to settle for less than the very best! I did not see that cause anywhere. I experienced a mixture of feelings and emotions. On one hand, the desire to continue fighting a tougher fight to conquer my son and help him overcome all those trespasses I was seeing with my physical and spiritual eyes. On the other hand, the defeat and disappointment of the ideal that I was fighting for was not real; it was the opposite. How did this happen? There was unbelief in my heart. I refused to accept the hurtful truth my life was experiencing with my son. I did not have feelings or emotions anymore. I felt like a zombie, walking and doing things, but with no heart in me anymore. I became distant and indifferent. I only answered when called or yelled at. I can relate this feeling to a mourning process. For me, it was a shocking experience, but I did not have the time or opportunity to mourn the loss of the expected result of my hard work and effort put into my son. It seemed that the person he was presenting, I did not know. This was not my son. I rejected the idea of accepting what I saw in the beginning, but after so many replicas of the same common denominator—"I've spent all my money and need more, and do not care how you are going to come to my rescue"—I felt used and abused. However, after expressing my disapproval and disappointment of the abuse inflicted on me by my son, and of course, he pretending to accept his fault and promising not do it again, I tried to believe in my son one more time. I had to work harder, to climb higher and to jump deeper, because of the long tail I had behind me already. Since it hurt and took me more to accomplish the task of getting money to cover the shortage of his lack of responsibility, when I discovered that he used me again, because the objective was not accomplished, my desolation was bigger and irreversible. I stopped trusting him. No matter how he said it, I did not believe him anymore. Do not get me wrong, I love my son, but I realized that I was not important in his life any more, that he can do his things alone, and that I must step aside to let him be. That is what I did. We will see the end result of his performance in this life."

--Heather paused and looked straight at her close friend Lucy, as if asking her to proceed with her story. Sure enough, Lucy got up; Heather did not say more, and exchanged seats with Lucy. By now, it seemed that everyone there knew what that chair at the end of the table meant: "Their turn to share what was deep inside and was still hurting."

Our eyes were fixed on Lucy. She did not wait, but immediately started:

Chapter 12

My Teenagers

"Talking about sons, I will share about one of my sons. One day I came home to find all these teenagers in the garage of my house. They had musical instruments and recording devices everywhere. I had not seen these kids before. They were my son's friends. I did not know that my son liked music. Guess what, he and another boy his age were the singers. The visiting in my garage was very common and frequent. When my son turned 15, I gave him a gold and diamond chain with a pendant, a cross. It was unique and very special. In this case, my son kept it as a remembrance of his memorable 15th birthday. I believed and trusted my sons. On one occasion, some of my son's belongings were missing. My youngest son mentioned something that made us all believe that my middle son was being bullied or had older boys as his friends. When we found out that our son had given this chain to one of these older friends, we went to the boy's house and spoke with his parents. Guess what had happened? My son was playing video games with his friends, and the older boys wanted to bet money every time they played. My son did not have money, but he bet his shoes, his shirts and on that particular occasion, he bet his special, meaningful chain. In other words, that chain was worth $10.00 to him. The boy's parents did not want to accept that their son was doing this with younger kids. They tried to defend their son. It was the obvious and right thing to do, I understand, but this was an abuse, because the betting was for $10.00, and the older boy took advantage of the situation. He had seen my son's chain, and he brought it to my son's memory to bring it to the betting game. It happened that the older boy had already sold it, and not for $10.00, but for over $1,000.00, and that other person had sold it as well. In other words, we were never going to get the famous chain returned to us. We were very upset at my son for not giving the appropriate value to things and for gambling them away. The older boy, who was a gambler with whatever he found to bet with younger kids, was never welcomed to our house again. My son understood that and respected our decision. Just a couple of months later, that older boy was killed on the street. According to rumors of people, this boy kept doing the same thing with other younger kids. The parents were visited by several younger kids' parents, but the older boy's parents kept defending their son's abusiveness with those other kids. According to what was said, one of those younger kids' brother, was not happy with the outcome of the parents' efforts to recuperate what was basically stolen from their house and decided to take revenge on his hands, and this older boy lost his life in the fight. It did not have to get to this extreme. If only the parents had cooperated with the other parents' requests, but of course, it is too late now. My son stopped the betting video games playing. He became more careful and responsible with his things. He kept meeting with his same-age friends and the love for his music increased to the point that he recorded a CD and went to music school. To this day he keeps writing songs, and he has a beautiful voice. He loved music even before he was born.

I had a wonderful experience when I was expecting him. I was seven or eight months pregnant. I used to go to this small church. This particular day, I was wearing a dress that my husband had given me as a present for Mother's Day. I loved that dress. It was light blue with white dots and stripes. I felt very comfortable in it. There was a special program at church. When the pastor was praying for the youth at the altar, he went to pray for the piano player who was his son. All of a sudden, I felt like someone had lifted me up, and my feet felt like they were made of gum because they were so flexible and I was dancing, but I would better say jumping so high that my husband, who was next to me, tried to hold me down. He kept saying: "You are pregnant, you are pregnant, and you cannot be doing this." And yes. My son loves music. Some times in the middle of the night or real early in the morning, he will be singing and writing his music. He is splendid with people. He is compassionate and loves God with all his heart. He is very spiritual. He has dreams and meditates on things that matter. I love my son.

My youngest son was supposed to be born on a particular date, but he decided to come to this earth two weeks later. With him I had another unique experience while I was pregnant. One day, while I was seven months pregnant or so, I woke up in the middle of the night. I was 100% awake. Not sleepy at all. All of a sudden the Holy Spirit talked to me in a way that my thoughts were in this conversation: "Lucy, fast." I immediately recognized that this was the Holy Spirit. Ok. I said. But, I quickly emphasized: "I am pregnant." I thought that the fasting was going to consist of something that I liked to eat, or juices, something like that. So, what am I fasting of? I asked. Dry, was the answer. What is dry? I asked. No food and no water, was the answer. I thought, well, I guess it is going to be just the morning or the afternoon. So, that prompted me to ask: "How long?" The answer was: "Three days." When do I start? I asked. The answer was: "Now." I said: "Okay." My fasting commenced at that time, meaning that I did not have breakfast, nor lunch. But, around 1:00 p.m., the regular hour to take my lunch, I felt famished. I went on my knees and prayed to God. I said: "You know that I am ravenous, I am pregnant, and you asked me to fast." As I was expressing my soul to the Lord, I felt my mouth so watery, it was something sweet as honey, I started crying, thanking God for His faithfulness, and I swallowed the sweet water. That sustained me until the end of the day. The next day, around 1:00 p.m., I was hungry and the above was repeated. The same thing happened the third day. I had no need of food or water. I was satisfied. My mother found out that I was fasting. She told the pastor at the church we were attending at that time. The pastor called me to his office and lectured me about my irresponsibility because I was pregnant and I could not put my son's life at risk. It was too late; that day was my last day of fasting. My husband and I chose a name for my son. However, one day after lunch, he moved inside of me so hard, and I could hear a name other than what my husband and I had for him. This name changing process of me hearing the new name repeated twice and three times while my son was active inside me. It was so clear and convincing, that when my husband picked me up from work, I told him my experience, and we decided to call him after the name He chose, and that is his name. He is a very smart, intelligent, responsible young man. He is a gentleman. I love him. He is my joy. He is my youngest son. I have had shattered dreams like everyone else, but I focus on the good things to bear life while I am breathing. What do you think?"

--Lucy gets up from the story telling chair and goes to the stove to get some of the goodies there. We think that she is going to proceed with her story, but she stays standing. As she sees our expectant looks waiting on her to continue, she says: "I am done, who is going to be next?" Finally, April, one of the more mature women there, takes the seat and moves it a little in a position to be able to see us all, and then she sits comfortably and says:

Chapter 13

Many Stages in One's Life

There are many stages in one's life, but some of them can leave scars forever. Childhood, adolescence, midlife, and adulthood. Basically, in each one of the different stages, there is something that is like a pillar to remember. Mine have been deep scars, but here I am still, trying to accomplish my calling in life. These last four, almost five years of my live, I have been like on a roller coaster, with the winds so strong that I cannot even hold on still. Sometimes I felt as if I was going to go overboard and be destroyed; I have especially felt lost, without direction. However, thinking back, I was warned years before. That is the only relief and hope that keeps me trying for a better tomorrow. I do not have control of the past. It is gone. The present, while involved in standing still and trying to make it better every time, I force myself to give the best of me in every situation. The future, I do not know if tomorrow will come. I live like there is a tomorrow, but maximizing the present.

Shattered dreams? While we are on this planet earth, we all are exposed to having our dreams shattered, some more than others, but it is the same common denominator. I am very passionate and give myself one hundred percent to what I do and others expect from me, especially when I give my word. My background could be a factor in this, but this is something that I have in me. I cannot go to sleep until I have covered my responsibilities for the day. Therefore, I expect others to do the same when it comes to them being responsible to me. When I say my background, I mean the places of work where I have developed my responsibility factor. I worked at a savings and loan institution, started opening savings accounts, and ascended to basically being in charge of the mortgage department. Years later, I worked at a construction company. I was in charge of having the crews together for every job site, from ordering materials to collecting the checks. I also worked for a law firm. In all these jobs, the responsibility was a must. So, I am used to commitment and responsibility. That is, I guess what molded my character. I believe that life is very exciting and interesting, but we create our own disasters. When we are single, we are responsible for ourselves, but when we get married, we depend on the other as well. It is exciting to plan and create goals to accomplish together as a couple, then the kids come to form part of the family and the goals continue to expand and make the journey full of expectancy and adventure. But, when one fails on the responsibility assigned, the whole household tumbles; the load of the other is heavier, because that one person has to make up for the both of them. Everything is acceptable and doable for the love there is between the couple. However, when the shortcomings keep repeating over and over, it does not matter how much love there is in the midst of them, the one making up for the two, starts to complain. In the beginning, it is not that noticeable, but then it is, until it comes to a point where the person carrying the load of both does not care, and gives up. When that happens, it is really hard to believe in the one carrying the lighter load. I guess the responsible one assumes the role of flying with the wind, or letting go and does not bother about whatever may happen with all the other things, goals and dreams built together for a better future. The easy going, lighter load-carrier, does not notice that the companion in life has given up, and keeps leaving the load for the other to keep carrying as done in the past. But, when the easy going comes back and finds the load in the same place where it was left, starts questioning: "What is going on?" Then, starts blaming the responsible one: "How come you did not do this, or that?" Until the moment comes when the one tired of failed promises and carrying the package that belongs to both of them, finally speaks up and let out all the feelings of inconsideration and abuse felt inside for such a long time. There are two options left: Either the short-comer shapes up and picks up all the mess created by self, and comes up to the standard of the other, or forgets about everything, leaves the mess the way it is and flies.

I am sure the responsible one will pick up the pieces and create a new journey, happy and excited, knowing that one day a brighter tomorrow awaits somewhere in the universe.

Shattered dreams? There are some people whose speciality is just that: To shatter people's dreams. However, it is not up to the person who likes making people miserable, but up to the person whose pieces of the puzzle are scattered all over, to pick them up and start a new dream. No one's life is in perfect harmony. There is always something missing. That is the only way we can relate to each other in this world. There are some who pretend to have it all put together, but I wonder if those are the ones who suffer the most when alone in the quietness of themselves. Life is so short to be pretending. It is much better to be real and open. Whoever is comparable to you, will come along and be willing to walk the paths of life with you. There are many paths, many people going in different directions, with different goals and dreams. Who, among all these people will be the one that will be your soul mate? It is just a matter of time. Time is the best friend and at the same time, the worst enemy. When you are young, time is on your side, our grandmas say; But, when we are at certain age, we do not want to talk about time, because it does not do us any favors. People say: "It does not matter where you go. If you have not changed your way of seeing life, you will bring the same problems wherever you go." It depends, because sometimes a change is a good thing to do. Maybe you will find the person who will help you with your load in this life in that new place, or make a change in someone else's life. God puts in us the desire and the way to do things. There is always a purpose for everything. Some of us may have experienced premonitions, some say, as to the future or our destiny in life. This is not a regular subject among human beings. Every day we find people reading books, journals of famous people to do or be like them. However, if you think about it, each and every one of us has a unique destiny and mission in life. The blessing among all people is that some find the right way, and some, even though it is presented to them; they choose to select the wrong one. There are many paths that we encounter on our journey through this planet earth, but which one do we take? In every stage in life, we are confronted with that past that for one reason or the other, we try to avoid or pretend that did not exist in our lives. However, the longer we try to avoid confronting it or facing it, the longer it will take for us to be free and enjoy life. Our shattered dreams begin even before we are born, because some of us were not the fruit of love, but of rape or a night of passion. It does not matter how we were conceived, or the circumstances in which we made the arrival to the family of which we are a part. What really matters is how we confront our battles and piece together the puzzle of the broken or shattered fragments left from those great and wonderful dreams we had. We are like butterflies, full of color and desire to be someone in life one day. We make pledges to serve society, the people around us. But, when we experience a great dissapointment, we tend to lower our expectations, rethink our plans and reinvent the wheel of life, thinking that we will be able to make it alone. We tend to isolate ourselves when we think that we are not capable of lifting up our eyes to see our deliverance coming over the horizons.

Shattered dreams? What exactly is that? We were created to dream and make things happen. Even though we do not understand our nature or the nature of things in our surrounding, time does not exist. We cannot go back in time, nor can we escape or fly into the future. Our reality is today. It is good to remember and tell the story to our present and future generations. Whatever hurt us at one point, it does not bother us in the present time telling the story. At that time when it happened, we thought that we were not going to survive the pain and that we were going to die. But guess what? We did not! That is exactly what happens to each one of us. We all can relate to that pain, as we all experience shattered dreams at one point or another in our lives while we are part of this illusion that is called: life on earth. It is just a dream of the real thing to come. We are just passing by, like the clouds in the sky. Every day the sun rises, and the sun goes down. Even though it seems that it does the same process every single day, what we experience is not the same. For instance, one day may be cloudy, another could be rainy, and the third could be sunny. We live so fast that we do not make time to observe the beautiful new mornings and sunsets. We live making plans and creating dreams that may not come to pass, and we become short of the most important thing in our assignment, observe and learn from the creatures surrounding us. Life is so very precious. We are in control of every single thing around us. The flowers are created to give us their beauty and aroma; each animal was created to our service and benefit.

However, we are scared of the lion and the snake. We have learned from our ancestors that they kill, so we automatically accepted that as the truth. Have we stopped to think that if we did not know that, maybe we would be living with them as we live with a cat or a mouse? We have these latter as pets, but we are scared of the former. What makes the difference between the beliefs we created, and the ones that others created for us? Does this mean that we are living someone else's ideas or dreams, instead of our own? Can we find the truth? This goes for each and every aspect of our life. We are uniquely and specifically created for a purpose. The thing that makes us upset or afraid could be the exact thing that we must conquer in our passing through this finite time on this earth. It could be like an assignment that we need to pass to make it to the real universe where we will be forever. We must have peace in our heart, in our being all the time, because Jesus gave us His peace before he left to prepare that heavenly place for us. So, anything we experience that is something other than peace, that may be the exact thing that we have to work on until we have it under our control. Each and every obstacle that we find destroying our peace, we must subdue. Have you noticed that each and every situation is so intense that it does not allow space for us to fight two at the same time? If it seems like it, it is because that particular one we are dealing with duplicates itself in a way that it seems that it is impossible to control. We probably deny it at first sight, then it magnifies with something else related to its original core, and then we are blown to fear, hate or disbelieve in ourselves. Meaning that seeing the problem at hand bigger than our ability, we are denying the all mighty power given to us by the Creator of the universe in ourselves. Therefore, by doing this, we are magnifying the problem and in our spiritual eyes we have been defeated. That is a lie. Therefore, we must see things the way they are and act upon each one of them with the reality that we know from our inside. We are more than conquerors in Christ Jesus, who did it all at the cross. He said that it was finished. All things have been given to us. Then?

Shattered Dreams. This is not a question, but an affirmation, because each and every one of us has experienced this at one point or another in our physical existence. Our lack of knowledge prolongs the suffering and the healing of our wounds. It also extends the wait to react to facts and commence picking up the pieces to start fresh all over again, or continue with whatever may have been left from the original dream we created. We deal with two different and opposing forces. One, to make us whole, and the other, to destroy our creativity and ability to accomplish those goals. Once we realize that, our healing process starts the motion of becoming part of that puzzle and the story that we will leave to our generations to come. God created us in His own image. He gave us the authority and the power over all things. Our lack of this knowledge, better yet said, our unbelief makes us stumble and fall short of the glory created by the infinite Glory of God. We are on this earth, in this physical body to reflect the Glory of God within His magnificent creation. We are His beings, created to enjoy and love the things He made for us. However, we live so fast that we do not make the time and take things as they are supposed to be. We magnify everything and become victims of our own creation. It does not make sense, but that is exactly what we do. Again, the lack of knowledge makes us hurt ourselves. We don't want to do that, and we fight to avoid suffering in the world, but yet, we self-inflict that which we are running away from. There is a reason for everything. It does not matter if we see good or evil. In the end, everything works together for good. That which we went through makes us stronger and brings us to our senses to be wiser and be able to teach others the lessons learned, for them to avoid stumbling on the same obstacle we did. Unfortunately, we cannot make anyone to be pain-free on this earth. We all have to go through something not that pleasant, in order to mature and have the experience that those bumps we encounter in life can give. That is the process of growing up to the standard that God wants to have us in order to use us. We all have a mission to accomplish to correlate with the universe around us. There is a reason we have the parents and siblings we have, the place where we were born, the place or places we visited and moved to. Even though we regret some events in our lives, there is always a purpose behind each and every one of them. After a while, when we look back and start seeing the puzzle of our life take shape and form, we realize that without passing through that valley - when we felt that we were not going to make it, because it was so painful that we decided to die at that time, we would not have been where we are in the present stage of our life. Then, and only then, we thank God and praise Him, because He was with us the entire time. Our pain is turned into joy, and we start dancing. We realize that if it had not been for that, we would had not moved to that place where we met our partner in life, and then, our children would not have been enjoying the fruit of our efforts together. Or, maybe we would not have encountered that angel personalized in a person whom we encountered during the time that our life was in danger, and during the process of helping us, talked to us in a way that we were able to see things differently. Our lives changed direction and made it through to the right path. Now we became aware of the truth and came to the conclusion that if that encounter had not happened, who knows where we would have been by now, because for sure, we were determined to take the wrong way. Do you see why we must think and thank all those stumbling blocks in our lives?

Shattered dreams? Many times. But, as they say, this is the way of life while in this physical body on this earth. Everywhere we go, every person we meet has a story, and as we listen to them, there is always a shattered dream and broken spirit somewhere. The "should haves and ifs" come about in the conversation. The life of each and every one of us is shaped in the way we pick up the leftover pieces of that shattered dream and broken spirit. Mine is not an exception. Actually, it is me telling you a story, so, mine must be the center of it, right? Some people say that we are the creators of our destiny. Do you believe that? Well, it could be true in a sense, but again, there are times when we do not have the energy or the desire to keep on going. The path ahead of us is completely uncertain, and sometimes we just want to give up. It is okay to sit down for a while to rest, but never to give up. While we have the breath of life in us, we must continue the fight until the end. We never know what the outcome of the story of our life will be. It does not matter how it started; the main thing is how it will end, and that we will not know until we get there. The circumstances shape us, but we should always be focusing on the beauty of everything that could possibly be. The flowers of the field teach us a lesson, to encourage us not to give up. There are different kinds of flowers for every season. Some of them, we can appreciate all year round. They give us the fullest of their beauty; they die, and again we can enjoy their aroma and color next season and so forth. We can admire the uniqueness of some beautiful and delicate flowers. They are typical of a particular period. We wait the whole year to have them around, and they last just for that specific time. So are we. Some of us are more sensitive and unique than others.

Some of us, people may think that there is nothing to be accomplished by us, but guess what? Our latest years are the best of all our existence. Some of us, our early years are the perfect and special ones of our life, and again, some of us could be the mid age. We have to find out under which category we fall. It does not matter if our splendor lasts for a few days, weeks, months or years. What matters is that we shine brightly, and our light enlightens the light of the people around us. That is what we must care and treasure with zeal. We must not allow our light to die before its designated time. Never give up. We could probably be just a few steps away from conquering the crown. We sometimes do not make it because of our lack of desire and dwindling enthusiasm of seeing life as it is. It is our turn to play in the show of life when we are walking this earth as Jesus once did. Where are we standing in the path to the main stage to perform our greatest piece of art assigned in the show of life? It does not matter. We must patiently wait; keep rehearsing the lines of our assignment. When the time comes to narrate our story, the Creator of the universe will align all the elements required to our best presentation. There are many spectators anxiously waiting for our turn in line. There may be some of us who want the best reward without the blood drops of sweat in Gethsemane. In fact, they want to avoid that scene and jump to the conclusion, when they say: "it is finished" Really? There is no such thing of being rewarded for a poor or not even lined up for the performance. Let us face it. There are some of us that yes; have passed the Gethsemane part, but in the middle of the road transfer the cross to someone else, and want to win the same reward. The applause and the crown of glory that are enjoyed and appreciated the most, are of those who went through the whole process, from choosing the twelve, eating the last supper, the blood drops of sweat in Gethsemane, the carrying of the cross all the way to Golgotha, feeling the loneliness of the last hour, until the long big loud scream: "It is finished". Wow, that is an accomplishment! That is a life well-lived, not wasting time and going for the shortcuts that life can offer. There are many of those shortcuts. However, in the end, when we cannot go back to reorder our steps, we are short of the glory, and our crowns are given to someone else. That is the sad part, that we suffered the same, we went through the same, but in the end, the reward is given to someone else. How come? We ask. That is not fair. Yes, you are right, but we all have the same opportunity. Except, that some are better equipped and informed than others. They did their hard and diligent work in the task of investigating and getting well informed before they made the decision to follow the steps of the big men and women all along the history of our existence. The sad part though, and one that we cannot take lightly, is that we cannot go back in time to do it better. We do not have a second chance. There are rehearsals on the way, but at the time of performance or those important decisions in life, when and where our roads form a cross, we only have one, that is one of the most important decisions of our entire existence. That is why we need to be well-informed and fit to declare what we must to and to make peace with whom we have to. There are no second chances in this regard. Even though our life on this earth is short, we have plenty of time to investigate and make our own conclusion. We have been taught that by our fruits they will know us. Then? Let us not fool ourselves with "perhaps and maybes." It is what it is, and that's all there is to it.

Shattered dreams? We all have them. So, let us stop blaming one another for the shortcomings of our failed tests in life. We are thrown quizzes once in a while. We may be happily celebrating our own or a loved one's birthday; we may be cutting the birthday cake. All of a sudden, that quiz is given to us. We receive a phone call that a loved one was involved in an accident. What are we going to do? Well, if we did our job, are well-prepared, we will pass the test. But if we are not, for sure we will fail it. How can you say that? How are you so sure of what you are saying? Well, because that is exactly what may happen, like it or not. How can we be well equipped and prepared? Doing these quizzes in our mind once in a while. Ask yourself. What would happen if this or that happened? How am I going to react? Really? Life is so generous with us to show us the scenarios of different tests that we will go through at one point or another during our existence. For example, look at the people in Indonesia or Japan. Some of them were having a great time, others were celebrating a birthday, and some doing nothing but watching TV. All of a sudden, the ground under their feet shook and they lost it all, family, friends, and their belongings. They were left alone with nothing; I mean nothing, not even an extra pair of underwear. What did they do? How were they able to keep living and going forward to be the survivors with the opportunity to tell their story to others? See? If they did it, we can also do it. That does not mean that our situation will be the same, or even similar. It is just a statement for your understanding, comparison and consideration. It could be almost an identical situation, but how are you going to react when calamity approaches your camp? God gave us tears to shed our frustrations and disappointments in life, to empty ourselves and to fill our hearts with hope and faith. He gave us encouragements to keep climbing that mountain with the cross on our backs until we get to the setting of our Golgotha, to inscribe the title on our cross: "Winner or Loser." Which one do you choose? Those are the only two titles. There is no almost, poor little thing. No... no... No... It is an either or it is an or. The choice is and has always been from the very beginning of creation, ours. That is right. We were given the instructions. It is up to us if we want to abide by them. We can fool ourselves in allowing others to design them for us, which is, of course, easier. We make shortcuts for ourselves, making sure we do not apply too much pressure. We don't want our tests to be either strong or long. We let our fleshly body tells us the pressure and the timing of the test. Really? Jesus himself wanted to go the other way around, but in the end He said: "Not my will Father, but yours." Meaning, the real way of carrying that cross. He did not die one second before, or one second after. The pressure and the timing were both in alliance and perfect. Let us choose the genuine and sincere way of living on this earth, and leave a legacy of honor to our generations to come."

--But where are your shattered dreams, April? We asked. She slowly got up from the chair and said: "I have experienced a little of all the shattered dreams you experienced, but I wanted to give echo to Lucy's way of seeing life, focusing on the good things that life has to offer." We learned a new perspective to make our loads lighter, and with hopes to a better tomorrow. We thought that everything was said for the day, but Candy got up, and went to the appointed chair, and said:

Chapter 14

Months went by, and nothing was happening

"Every day we learn something new. I always believed everything my family said because I wanted to trust that everything they did and said was in our best interest. However, I have also discovered that it is not always the case, not every time. I opened my own business and worked hard to make it prosper, but ever since I did that, the income started to become less and less, to the point that I had to borrow money. My father and my mother sent me whatever they could. I never realized how much $20.00 could be appreciated. When you are in need, that is a lifesaver, we say. There had been seven years in the wilderness. In looking for green pastures, my friend invited me to try her company. I closed my eyes and gave my all to make it work. Even though deep inside of me, that quiet and smooth voice was telling me not to do it. Again, I went ahead and did it anyway. But, I was promised so many different things, that I thought I had made the right decision. Three months went by and nothing was happening. Actually, the first week I was with them, on a Sunday morning, I woke up; I was not dreaming, but I distinctly heard the voice that I am so familiar with, the Holy Spirit, saying: "Open your own business." I was determined to do so, but again, my friend rebuked me. She kept saying that I was ungrateful because I did not appreciate all the referrals I was receiving from the company, etc. Since I was living in her house, I did not want to argue, so I dampened my spirit and kept trying. However, every time I made a phone call to a possible new client, or I was on my way out the door, I felt this heavy anxious sensation, which evidently was not peace. I did not have energy, and that feeling was dragging me down. I made up my mind different times, until one day I finally decided to give myself the opportunity to succeed in a different area. I am a broker. I studied hard to pass my license. I went through the whole process of getting my permits and have everything in order for my company to start blessing people. I do not know what it was; the building, the people, or if it was part of my destiny that everything went the opposite of my expectations, but there I was.

I have learned to have the best, and at the same time, not to have anything. I was sleeping on the floor. The apartment was on a busy street corner. It was so difficult to sleep because the noise was too loud. But, we get used to everything with time. Sure enough, the noise did not bother me anymore. I went to the city to get a permit to work from home. I was fortunate enough that it was given to me right away. In fact, they suggested to me that I could pay the required fee in three payments, which I gladly accepted. I was thinking: "One day I will be able to have that marvelous house, and that big office for my business. In the meantime, I cannot complain because I have a roof over my head and the support of my husband, I mean, financial and spiritual support." I could not say the same about my kids because if I did not call them, they did not make an effort to do so. My brothers and my sisters called me once in a while asking me if I was okay. One of my sisters even asked me for my bank account number to deposit some cash, she said, but I never received any money from her. You know, we cannot count on someone else's financial help, or any other favor, because it may be more disappointing than the movies and the soap operas on TV.

It is so refreshing and rejuvenating when we have been liberated from the heavy load that we thought had no limit, or that it was impossible to break free from the burden and the stress implied in whatever sircumstance or sitution we are in. We were born to be free, and to grow to our maximum potential, but the environment we grow up in and the relatives around us minimize our capacity to expand and be prosperous. We do not say many things, we observe, and even want to scream and say what we really think, but we stay quite. Sometimes, it is best according to the circumstance, but other times we do not say anything because of fear. When that is the case, freedom is more appreciated and applauded. This event makes us stronger and more courageous. Nothing is compared to a clear and free mind and spirit. As you may have realized, we live one day at a time. This does not mean that we do not have our dreams and goals, but in order to get to where we want to be, we must go one step at a time. Each day brings its battle to fight. But, please do not get me wrong, we do not wrestle everyday. No. There are some times when we have that peace and rest that our body and soul need to get the strength after a debilitating journey of days, or prior to a strong confrontation in the battlefield. Every single day is different and unique. We must struggle and fight to make it a plus in our book of actions on this earth. We must accomplish our goals for that particular day. We cannot be dismayed and overwhelmed with the test for the week, or month. One day at a time is how we will win the war ahead of us. We carry all the hurts and disappointments from our past, and we may not realize what day it is or what happened the day before. This does not mean that everyone is the same. There are some charismatic people who know what they are doing. Their program is set, and they do not care who will fall. They are determined to get where they want to be; they do not care who they step over or push aside. Let us be careful with this situation, because we cannot accomplish something and celebrate the victory at the suffering or expense of others. We are a reflection of that other person in front of us. Why are we at peace with certain people? Why is it that there are people whom we scarcely know and seldom encounter at the store or the school, yet we do not like them? Something in our being rejects them. We ask ourselves: But why do I feel this way? I do not even know this person. We question ourselves and are hard on ourselves. It is normal that sometimes we feel this way. Each and every person we encounter on our path through this physical existence is a reflection of ourselves, and we must conquer something in order to get to the next step on that ladder of success and freedom. What causes us to feel either way, at peace or not liking someone? Could it be that the same things that we hate in those people are our own weaknesses? Our heart is deceitful. Not everything that we think is bad; it is actually how we perceive it to be. Let us think of this situation as if we had all things upside down. We cannot really appreciate things as being ordinary like others do, as we are accustomed to our way of seeing things. Our physical eyes and ears are very tricky. Sometimes we see things, but they are so distorted, that we see them as being bad, when in reality they are very useful. Why? Because what we see badly, it is predestined for us, to make us mature and grow.

Our experiences in life promote inner-growth. It does not matter how early in life we learned of this other side of the perfect life expectancy with which we are born. What an irony, that the people whom we trust the most and think we are safe with, the people whom we believe are the ones who have our best interest at heart and would want our prosperity and well-being are the ones in most of the cases who are responsible for our first shattered dreams in this life. Unfortunately, we perish because of lack of knowledge. But who will teach us? What is it that we want in life? If we are just going to be whining and complaining about our circumtances and about who is responsible for our distress and suffering, believe me, there will be no teacher in the world who would be capable of doing miracles with these kind of people. On the other hand, if you are trying to find the ways out of your situation and are not focusing on the past because you are smart and know that it does not matter how hard you cry or how loud you scream, you will never be able to fix the past. If you are that kind of person, then there is hope and help for you. The universe accommodates all the paths in front of you to meet the right person who will guide you through the right direction. Not only that, but the Holy Spirit who dwells inside of you will start communicating with your spirit to bring you to the truth. That truth that you have been searching for is already there, even if for some reason you think that it is taking too long or you feel that it is never going to come. Do not despair, when you find the truth and experience the freedom of your spirit, you are not going to even remember the tears or suffering; your sadness will be transformed into dancing, the happiness that your heart and being will experience at that time will surpass any pain or negativity you have ever experienced in the past. Believe me. It does not matter what it was, the reason for it, or how shattered your dreams and broken your spirit were. This is the beauty of the second opportunity. This opportunity is given to the over-comers of the little misfortunes. In other words, let us say for the purpose of illustrating this idea. You were put to a small test. As you passed this test, a bigger assignment is given to you to develop yourself and to achieve a goal. We think that some tests are easier than others. That is why the easy assignments do not take long for us to accomplish. Then you get some that are not hard, but for some reason, possibly the people around us or the obstacles we have to overcome cause us to take longer. It feels that they are boring and tedious and that we would prefer to pass them on to someone else. Unfortunately, we have to deal with each and every task that challenges us. That is our mission on this planet earth. Therefore, my suggestion is that we should find the sunny side of things to make this life a happy journey. Instead of focusing on the thorns we find on the way, it would be better to admire the roses so we can have the beauty and the pleasant smell of them on the thorny path ahead of us in that particular stage of our life. The blessing of this is that nothing is forever, and each stage we experience is for a season only. So, let us hold on tight and know that everything will pass. Either we make our journey more livable, or we are going to feel that we are in hell, because we are rejecting the thorns on that part of the road. Even though it is just a short distance that we will experience the discomfort, we are defensive and rebel against the inevitable, making the pain more intense and the time that we will experience this discomfort seem forever. Do you understand the point? If we have to go through the tunnel, why fight it? It is better to recognize the place, accept the situation, and relax. Nothing is forever, so it will be for a season. After that, we will confront a new giant. Every time we encounter and accept the challenge life sets in front of us, the next one will be easier, or at least, we have gained valuable experience from the past and are better equipped and more ready to handle the next dilemma. Head-on? Yes, head-on, because now we know better. Right? Why do I tell you this? Because I have learned to see the flowers in the midst of the thorns in the different fields and valleys I have had to cross in my life, so you may have a better chance to make it to the other side with less scars in your heart"

--We all looked at each other in a quiet and thoughtful shared spirit. As it was the turn of the elders of the group to share their stories, we noticed that there was more wisdom and life experience we could learn from, so we were eager to hear what Genesis had to say. Slowly she approaches the famous chair. She asks for a pillow to put on her back; as Ana hands it over, my mom brings more cookies, and coffee to the table. Genesis starts:

Chapter 15

Different Roles Played in Life

"But, wait. It hurts, it is so embarrassing. Where do I start? I played so many different roles in life. I do not remember when was the last time that I genuinely loved myself, if I ever did. I have to dig so deep into myself that I do not know where to start.

I warn you, it won't be easy in the beginning. It will hurt sometimes. I already heard one of you to say that it is okay to cry at times, so please, bear with me.

A lie casts a shadow over your inner light preventing it from shining and will eventually extinguish it completely until you are left in utter darkness.

The truth, on the contrary, enhances your light until it reaches its maximum brightness and keeps it shining for generations to come.

Only you decide to take this beautiful journey of discovering yourself just the way you are. As you are doing this, you might discover some wounds that are still bleeding, and they may take more effort and time to accept, forgive, and heal. Please know that no matter the wounds, they will heal, and you will go on with life again to encounter the next one and the next one, until you get out of the dark tunnel and see the light again, or for the first time, if that is the case. So what, there is nothing to lose, the dreams are already broken. What we are looking for is to pick up the pieces that are left, and see what we can bring to life in a new beginning. We will go step by step through the minefield until we get to a safe and better other side.

Who does not have shattered dreams?

It is hard to face reality and accept the fact that we all do. It does not matter what our social standards are, the status we carry, or the rank of the family into which we were born; there are always broken dreams. There is a shattered dream in each one of us. But, "why?" we scream. Well, just imagine if some of us were perfect, and some were among the less gifted of whose dreams were shattered. Can you picture the world we would be in? If all having the wings cut here and there, we live like cats, and dogs, envying what the other has, putting us down, etc.

These meetings are intended to make a pause in our busy schedule, discover the real human beings we were created to be, and accept our mistakes or shortcomings. We need to do this in order to grow to our maximum potential, with the many or few pieces left after the crash we encountered in the complex universe given to us for our discovery.

To start, we did not choose our parents, siblings, or to be the only child if that is the case. What about our height or the color of our skin, just to name a few of our characteristics. We did not have any input in the matter. Then? Why are we complaining about the very first essence of our existence?

We would think that there is an answer for everything, but is there really?

There is no manual to a perfect life. But, our experience is a contribution to ourselves, to take life as it is and live the rest of our lives to the fullest, without regrets, and most of all, free of shame and condemnation. How does this sound?

From every situation, good or bad, we learn something to use to our advantage in the future.

It is good to review the past scenes of our life, especially the ones that scarred us, the ones we even avoid thinking about.

What happened?

Was he your father, your brother, your uncle, a family member, or even your boyfriend?

Yes, you trusted him, and he, in essence, killed your dreams. For each one of us the situations and circumstances were completely different, but brings us all to the same spot, the wounded field. Some of us are already healed, some are in the recuperating stage, and some are just in the emergency room where they were just admitted, because it just happened to them today. You see, you are not alone, and you are not the only one as you probably thought. We all need each other to make it to the other side of the tunnel. Except that there are those who are healed and willing to share how they were wounded, and there are those who are constantly bleeding from the deep cuts in their heart and soul, but do not know who to trust and be helped, and of course, there are those who bear the huge scars, but are closed up and are not willing to share their story with anyone, not even with themselves; they are in the denial field. How did their wounds heal? I do not know, but maybe because they did not get the proper help, the wounds healed in a way that the scars are not normal, and are so obvious. That is why they try to hide them. So, they are still in need of a plastic surgeon to be entirely free, because when you are not comfortable with what you see in your being, something is not quite right.

Would you be willing to share at what stage you currently find yourself?

Our goal is to dance in both the sunny day and the rainy days. It does not matter the situation; we must be in control of it.

--- Time does not wait. Every minute counts, and we must make the difference.

Just think of this, maybe you were wounded when you were just a little girl or boy. Perhaps by now you are already an adult. Maybe because of what you went through, you are afraid of marriage and having children. Do you see the point of time? You are wasting yourself by being caught in the past as if the clock stopped for you at that specific tragic moment. Can you just imagine for a minute how life would be if that scene in your movie had never happened and you were just the perfect you? How your life would be? What was your dream in life? Maybe you had dreamed of being married and having four or five children, or maybe eight or twelve kids. What was your dream? The point that we are trying to emphasize here is that there was a time in your life when you had a dream for your future, but because you were forced by circumstances and events outside your control, your dream was shattered and broken in a million little pieces, or so you tell yourself. How in the whole wide world am I going to mend my broken heart and make something new out of all these little tiny pieces? Well, since we already know what your original dream was, the pieces still have the essence of the great plan that you were called for in this life. Therefore, the universe recognizes the particulars of that original idea you had for your life. Because you took control of the situation again, everything that was going wrong and in different directions resolves itself. Because the commander in charge was wounded and was lead to believe that his or her life was over, all of a sudden a new idea comes to mind, hope glimmers, and the whole universe rushes to bring you the means you need to develop a new plan and enables you to achieve your goals with what you have in hand. Your assignment on this earth will be completed. The shattered dream that left you disabled and wounded will now be developed by you being strengthened, renewed and determined to change your sorrow into dancing in the rain of blessings that you cannot contain, but you have to shout with all you have in your inner being for the world to know and the whole universe to confirm that even though you still have the scars of the past, you are making use of those same scars to be successful and triumphant the rest of your life. Actually what happened to you and scarred you is precisely the pinnacle of your liberation and accomplishment of your realization as the human being that you were created to be from the very beginning. Just think of this. Without scars, there is no reward. Do you agree?

It does not matter what happened to you. Would you like to face it and talk about it?

- Were you raped? Sexually abused? Betrayed? Taken advantage of? Did you lose your house, your family...? There are so many different other things that you could have gone through. Just the fact that we are talking about this that hurt you so much and you had hidden so deep in your heart, is a plus. We are making progress. CONGRATULATIONS!

Just consider that you were given a mirror in your right hand; you must see yourself even though you do not want to do it because it hurts. Little by little you are overcoming this first steps, then you will be able to talk about it and help others do the same; free themselves from the heavy chains of condemnation and guilt to the green pastures of acceptance and redemption.

No matter what the circumstances were that caused you to be marked so deep for so long, please know that while there is that breath of life in you, there is hope. Say that every day. We know that you are not alone in this battle. Each and every one of us on this planet earth has the same stigma of having their dreams shattered for different reasons and circumstances. So, the job of recouping the leftover pieces will be much easier. You are not alone in the picking up of whatever is left of you.

- We must understand that the blaming and pointing fingers at everyone around us is not going to help. We cannot go back in time, and killing that person or persons whom you blame for your disgrace is not going to take you anywhere. Yes, you bring them to your memory to realize and recognize that fact, but mainly to forgive them. No matter how much it hurts and how many times you have to cry, those tears help you clean your soul and heal the wound. The scar will be there for the rest of your life, but it will not hurt anymore. Therefore, we agree that since we do not have any other choice in this difficult dilemma, we decide to forgive those that we blame for our hurts and shattered dreams.

Now that we forgave others, it is time to look in the mirror and see ourselves just the way we are, all scarred and worn out, tired and weak, but alive! That is what matters. Alive!!!

- We now must forgive ourselves. Yes, you are right, victims often blame themselves for causing the damage done to their lives. So, since there is nothing you can do because you cannot go back in time, you do not have any other option but to forgive yourself. It may take you a while to look at yourself and accept the fact that you are forgiving your stupidity, your rebellious heart, whatever you may have called yourself for that past. It is okay, forgive yourself.

Now that you have forgiven yourself,

- You must embrace that forgiveness. Remember, you are alive, and you deserve a second chance. Besides, there is nothing you can do to correct the past. Whatever damage was done is done, and there is nothing that you or anyone in the entire universe can do to change that. Therefore, we accept the forgiveness, and we will never condemn ourselves, ever again. We are free and ready to start our next task.

What about those who feel that there is no hope or mercy for themselves anymore? Perhaps you believe that no one else has committed the transgressions against your neighbor like you have. You feel that there is no coming back from the dark shadow that you have entered into. You may even think that the tunnel of despair and terror is so deep, and you are so lost in it, that you might as well keep doing what you know best to do; deceive, destroy and kill. You may even say to yourself: "Maybe if I had known this when I was just starting to hang around with my friends on the streets, when there was still hope for my life, but now it is too late." Please let me tell you that it is never too late. If you have stayed with us thus far, you are screaming for help. Yes, there is help, even though you would prefer not to hear those statements, because this means that you have to recognize what you have done and call it by its name. I know, it is so hard and painful to even think about it, but it is part of the path to freedom. Once you start not to deviate from your thoughts, from the scenes of your past where you are seeing yourself doing the shameful acts you are not proud of, this is the new beginning for your coming back from hell itself. Let me warn you. It is not going to be easy, especially when you pass through those valleys of death, when you are alone with yourself, with no friends to distract you from seeing reality just the way it is. Sometimes instead of admitting what we did wrong, we try to justify ourselves by focusing our attention on the things or people around us, so to find a reason why we did what we did. We end up believing that we were the victims of the circumstances and that we just reacted in self-defense. Is it really true? Do we really believe that? We are the only ones who know exactly the motivation and the instincts that moved us to commit such abominable mistakes in our live. We do not want to see ourselves in the mirror. There are so many horrible things that we are afraid and ashamed to see. Let me tell you something. No matter how far we go and how fast we run from reality, the past will always hunt us and bring us to accounting of the right and wrong we have done. There are some people who reinstate themselves by inflicting pain to their body through different sacrifices. At least that is what the intention is, and that is what they believe. They think that by doing that, they have been redeemed from their misery and the pain of their guilty conscience. There are some who are such good actors, that in the movie they chose to play, they live in such a perfect harmony and paradise, where they pretend to ignore the past like it never happened. They reinvent their lives; they are just perfect. Nothing of the past is real, it happened to someone else, not them; to the point that they get lost in the midst of so many different personalities they adopt. They do not know who they are anymore. They try to hide in drugs, alcohol and in many other degrading obscurities that surround us in every corner of life. They avoid being alone with themselves. They have to be loud so they do not have to hear the cries of condemnation and painful wounds of their shattered dreams. They live a lie pretending not to have any wounds, to the point of being numb to pain. They have learned to cheat everyone, including themselves, and that is the most painful and sad reality human beings can experience in their lifetime. Unfortunately, when our body does not respond and we are in physical pain, when the struggles of sickness and desperation of life overwhelm us, we may find ourselves by force of illnesses, bedridden in a hospital or at home alone. It is then that as much as we want to avoid the past, it presents itself uninvited, it forces us to face it, and it imposes itself on us. We want to cover our eyes, we have them closed to the physical realm, but that is when we see 1000 times more clearly in a dimension where nothing is hidden from our sight. There is no place to hide. We see everything with such a bright light that there is no confusion. Yes, we are there, and we are the ones who inflicted pain to that person who died. Yes, we witnessed the rape of that poor teenager, and because we were scared, or wanted acceptance in that group of cool guys or girls, we did not say anything. Yes, we were the ones who stole that merchandise and let people to believe that it was done by someone else; we put the blame on that humble and honest man who ended up in jail because of us. Yes, we were the ones who took advantage of the trust of our best friend and got involved with the wife or the husband of such best friend. And yes, we were the ones to blame for so many other shameful acts.

It is then that we realize that we cannot escape the past. We have to face it, but sometimes it is too late because it comes to us so strong that it suffocates us. It may even knock us down with a sudden ailment that leaves us disabled for the rest of our lives, with no hope of redemption because we will never be able to recount our steps and pick up the pieces of our shattered dreams. What a sad way to end the story of our lives on this earth, where we were placed to conquer the attacks of our self-depraved mind. Thank God you are here and are given the opportunity to stop, to think and be able to do something to end your days on this earth at peace with yourself and others around you. Because when you are not at peace with yourself, you hate everyone, and that is not good; we need each other in order to be the one hundred percent that we were meant to be. There is nothing wrong with being mistaken at one point in life. Remember, we all have shattered dreams. The rewarding thing is when we recognize that our dreams were shattered or broken in one thousand pieces, and accept that by picking up the pieces, something beautiful, unique, different and special will be created to be useful in life, to help others in the journey to perfect inner peace and freedom, where we all be transformed and be able to change our mourning and sorrow into dancing. It is then, and only then, that we will not care about the scars we all have of the shattering of our dreams, because the joy in our hearts will be greater than the pain inflicted by our shattered dreams. Hallelujah! Aren't you excited?

What about the other side: Were you the one inflicting pain? Were you the one who assaulted, the sexual abuser, or.....?

What about you? Maybe you were incarcerated, and you are paying for what you did. Even though this is what society and the law say, you feel that this is not enough, or maybe you feel that this is enough because you paid with time in jail. But, what do you feel? What do you say? Do you still feel guilty and have not forgiven yourself for what happened? You keep saying: If I had only done things differently, or I should have done this or that. As you know, those are words that basically do not exist in time, because you just cannot go back and start all over again. Perhaps you did not even know the person on whom you inflicted pain, and maybe you do not feel guilty at all because you think that you are even with the world; you did your time in jail. Are you still single? Are you married? Different scenarios, different possibilities, only you know exactly what your situation is. Maybe your circumstances were not addressed in our meetings, but the idea may be there for you as well.

If you are single, just think that in this world and the universe, the law is the same. Treat others the way you wish to be treated. This encompasses both you and your loved ones. Let us think a little deeper and more consciously about what the future may bring for you. Time does not stop, it continues its course in life to pay back or to reward whatever the circumstance may be. The person who suffered because of you, directly or indirectly: Was she a young girl, a middle-aged woman, an elderly woman, or was he a little boy, a teenager, a middle-aged man, or an old man? Please stop to think that whatever the case was, that person could easily has been your sister, your mother, your daughter or your wife. But, if the individual was a male, we could be talking about your brother, your father, your son, and if you are a woman, we could be talking about your husband. Do you get the point that I am trying to make here? Do you remember how old that person was when the incident happened? With whom do you relate these possibilities? As we were saying before, time goes by so fast. We can neither slow it down nor stop it. Although we wished, but it is impossible. It is the law of time, and it will never change because it has been established so, and there is nothing anyone can do to the contrary. One day will come when you will fulfill all the roles defined above. It depends on your present stage, but we all play the different depictions in life. The little girl or boy, the sister or brother; with its exception if you are the only child. Afterward, we face the responsibility of a mother or father. Again, with its own and unique exclusions of those barren. Later we face the golden years when we became grandparents. Undoubtedly, with its non-inclusions, but for the illustration of the cycle of one's life determined for the humans on this planet earth. Now, can you see more clearly what damage you did to that family whose member was inflicted pain? Did the victim die? ...

Let us pause here a little bit. Please think! What would you have felt if you were the mother or the father of that little girl or boy? Yes, we are getting closer to the heart of your own territory. If you have a child of your own, you can feel the pain. What if that person was your sister or your brother? What then? Can you relate? Or what if that person was your mom or dad? You know more or less the age of the person when you recall what happened. But what if that person was your husband or wife, it depends on your case, and if that person was your grandpa or grandma? Can you see the big picture now? That is why it is imperative to be at peace with your inner self. We do not want that cycle to be repeated in your lifetime, but worse, within your family members. I pray that you understand the importance of these heartfelt words and be willing to make the difference. Break the chain of consequences, be free and make your loved ones free of your past wrong doings and inevitable retributions. They do not deserve to go through the same, but in a magnified percentage of what that person suffered at your own hands. Remember? Is it worth to be still and do nothing to change the future of your descendants in the catena of sequels of your acts of the past? It does not matter how old you were when it happened. The point is that you were involved in the act, and the person that you love or will love the most will redeem the price or reward of your actions. What do you say? Don't you think it is better to stop for a minute or two and reflect on the thing or things done? You can ask the victim if that individual is near you and alive to forgive you. If that is not the case, perhaps that being is far and you do not know where this person might be; he or she might have passed away. In reverence and with your heart in your hand ask God to forgive you, and of course, you have to forgive yourself and bless that person whose life and dreams were shattered because of you. Declare to the universe that the chains of condemnation and retribution of your past wrong-doings are broken and will not be repeated in your generation because you put constraints on your past, and every one of your loved ones are free.

Thank you for your honesty, and if you would like to share your story, please do so. I am sure you will be a blessing to many who may relate to you by your sharing, and it will encourage them to break the chains of their past as well.

What about those who inflict pain to themselves? They are rebels among the sheep. Everyone thinks: "Why is this person the way he or she is? His or her family is of good standing among society, the parents are professionals, in fact, all the family members are of good reputation and well educated. Why is this person the only one who brings shame to the family?" Are you the black sheep? Why? What happened? What are your stumbling blocks?

Have you felt like an outsider among the family assigned to you? Sometimes we have a competitive spirit and do not want to be left behind. We want to be the smarter one; the number one. We see our surroundings and feel challenged to a higher level. We judge ourselves short of what it is required to conquer the objective. Therefore, we want to get the attention of others, but in the opposite direction, harming ourselves. It does not make sense, but that is exactly what we do. Have you seen boys and girls caught up in drugs, alcohol, and prostituting themselves? It seems that they like to embarrass their parents and family members; it is like they don't mind being hated by society. It does not have logic at first sight, but when you start discerning, you come to realize that these people were neglected on someone's way to success. They want to be different to what they are accustomed to seeing every day; a neat dresser, a healthy diet, a well-organized schedule, the best schools, the well behaved brothers and sisters, cousins and the perfect parents you would think. ....

Have you stopped to think the reason for this contradicting behavior in an environment where you would expect the best outcome of such individuals?

Well, it is not rare, and this may shock you, but have you ever thought that within that beggar on the street, that prostitute, that drunk laying on the floor of that supermarket, there could be a great leader? Yes, there is a strong-willed character embodied in that person who started the idea of being different. They are not able to discern, and for lack of knowledge and advice, they fear sharing such thoughts of uniqueness, so they decide to go against the current of the standard norms imposed at home by those well put together around them.

Of course, being alone in such a task of changing the world, it takes great leader's ideals. Therefore, madness takes over and defeats the outward body of this person, leaving the inner self with such vast shattered dreams. What do we say? Shattered, broken dreams? At least that is what we see when we look at people like that on the streets. We, in our human way of thinking, predict that there is no hope for those homeless and forgotten beings on the benches of the parks, and everywhere society is ashamed to even pass by. It is as if they are contagious and we want to be as far away we can possibly be, not to even look at them. Why? ... Well, that is what we have been taught. You get together with the well behaved, the smarter, the best families, etc....

In the meantime, these great leaders at heart, little by little, are getting farther away from their reality and lost in the darkness of that tunnel where no one wants to be, finding themselves alone to die in their shattered dreams. They will never have the opportunity to share their stories, like us. They will never pick up the pieces of their shattered dreams to create new and better lives filled with accomplishments. They, like you and I, have been struck by the gale of resistance to accomplish their goals, and since they are a minority exposed to a triple opposition, not only of themselves, but by society and their families, their life expectancy is much shorter than yours and mine. Why? Because even though they are screaming for help in the way of helplessness, they can hardly move or speak. How can they look for help on their own? They are lost in their world; they do not think they need help. On the contrary, they believe that we are the ones who are crazy and need help. Can you believe this? But you and I know that the reality is such that we had not thought about this at all. Next time you approach a homeless person for whatever reason, please, I challenge you not to avoid the encounter, look at him or her at the eyes. You will see such sadness, and you will be able to hear the scream for help in your heart. If you are driving, stop your car and pay attention to those people in need. Have you ever thought for a moment why that person is in that situation? Can you imagine yourself just for a second in those shoes and in those clothes? That is what makes the difference. When we see and feel ourselves in other people's bodies, especially in those in need, that is when we can come to our senses and comprehend the magnitude of the Golden Rule to treat others as ourselves."

--Oh my God. Genesis, you are intense, Anna cheered. But, Christina immediately said:

Chapter 16

The Homeless People

"She is right. I will share with you something that happened to me some years ago.

I went to a Bible study, and we were taught about Jesus sometimes embodying himself in homelessness to see how we would react to find him in the least of the least among us. Well, this particular day was payday, and at lunchtime I went to the bank to make a deposit into my checking account. On my way back to work, I saw that people were going around a particular space. As I got closer to the area, I was able to realize why that was happening. The stinky smell of that homeless person sitting at the edge of a window at that hill of one of the streets in San Francisco, was the reason people were passing by as far as possible. The bus stop was right there in front of him. I immediately remembered what I had learned at church the night before. Even though my nose hurt at the burning stinky smell of that homeless person, I hesitated a little to stay, but I did. I was embarrassed to be the only one there by him. Everyone kept moving as far away from him as possible. I wanted to do my homework and practice what I was told to do. Little by little, I turned towards him and step by step got closer to him. He was sitting down with his long hair partially obscuring his face, looking down in a position of resignation, his shoulders down and his hands on his knees. He did not even care, nor was he aware of me approaching him. I stood next to him and said: "Jesus loves you." I was surprised that he heard me, because he nodded in acknowledgment. I continued telling him that he was born not to be in that situation, but maybe to be an attorney, a doctor or someone in society to help others. He nodded again. I asked him: "What is your name?" To my surprise, he replied. He told me his name was Michael, and I told him that I would never be able to forget his name, because my husband's name was also Michael. I went back to my spot, a few steps in front of him to wait for the bus. As I was waiting, I turned back to see Michael, and he looked at me. When he did, my body shook from top to bottom in an unexplainable way that I cannot to this day comprehend. All of a sudden, my heart was full of compassion and love for Michael. I wanted to help him, to do whatever I could to make him whole. I was praying for him. I was asking God to send angels to help Michael accomplish the task he was assigned to do on this earth, to bless him and to protect him. I just could not stop caring for Michael. I looked back again and saw him standing up as the bus was approaching our stop. I immediately got on the bus, paid for two fares, his and mine, and started making way for Michael to sit. When I turned to see him and tell him that I got a seat for him, Michael had disappeared; he was nowhere. I just could not control myself. I started crying; my soul was trembling. I realized that God had sent an angel manifested in the body of Michael. He just wanted to see how I was going to react to His presence as a homeless person. Let us be careful how we treat others, because you just never know if God Himself comes to you in the body of that person that you want to avoid. Let us be open and receptive to the different callings of help from our neighbors. We are here to help each other to accomplish our task on this earth. Let us help each other to pick up the pieces of our shattered dreams, clean up the wounds of our past to heal and to rejoice with the scars left for us to remember how strong and courageous we are."

--Christina gestured that she was done. Melinda was the first one to applaud and said:

Chapter 17

Lives Never Touched

"Congratulations! You are a Hero, not a bum. Always remember that!

Have you ever thought about those people whose shattered dreams left them all crumbled down? They just gave up and do not want to do anything to pick up those pieces to start a new dream. Actually, they want to get attention in provoking pity from others. They claim to be sick all the time, all the horrible things happen to them, they are the ones abused by others, all the bad things that you can think of occur to them. They create those incredible stories so to get the attention of people around them; and of course, when someone does not believe their tales, these pity craving people get upset and mad, to the point of getting physical with whomever holds up the mirror to face reality. We are in a world so beautiful and at the same time so complex. We live among so many different experiences people have gone through, that we could write books and books trying to discern the complexity of the different personalities, but we could never find a pattern to fit each one of them. We are so unique and special. The dream in each one of us was shattered for various reasons. Even though there may be some similarities, it will never be the same outcome, because some react a certain way, and some will just decide not to gather the pieces, and die just like that. Others, on the other hand, will try to make it and hold on until the end no matter what. These last ones make the world tremble and set the way for them to get to their destiny. This group knows where they are going and will not give up until getting to the top of their potential to fulfill their dream and plan assigned to them for their term on this planet earth. The universe aligns its means to bring about their wishes to life. Here we see the importance of knowing where we are going. There may be rain and fog, but nothing keeps us from finishing the race. We may be scared, but we will be triumphant giants in the end. We are the ones passing on the token to the generations to come. Our names will be mentioned as examples to follow by our descendants. The over-comers know the taste of the victory, as they feel on their flesh the price of each piece of the reward to their efforts. The defeated ones just talk about who they knew that went through something; they always talk in third person, they cannot relate to what it takes to be a leader. They wanted to, but they were not willing to pay the cost. In which group would you like to belong? Hopefully among the conquerors, but the decision is yours only.

I heard a missionary say: "If we could go through a cemetery and were given the opportunity to see the tasks assigned to each one of the people laying there, we would be shocked to see the many books never written, the songs never aired, the movies never taken to the big screens. The different lives never touched by the inspiration and gift given to each one of those people, who for many reasons were not able to overcome adversity and gave up for lack of knowledge or for lack of motivation." Would you like to be remembered as part of this last group? Again, the decision is only yours. There is no other way out. Each of us sooner or later at one point in our life must experience the shattering of our dreams, but the point is to be prepared to know what we are going to do about it.

If you would like to share your experience when you faced the shattering of your dreams, please do so. Whoever may relate to your story will be grateful for bringing more light to their paths.

Our shattered dreams are basically stepping stones that bring us closer to the goal or calling in our life on this earth. The family members assigned to us while we are on this journey through the venture of passing through this planet, are usually the ones who shape us better with their characters and mistreatments. They equip us to be ready to face our real problems. These present themselves as our partner, our in-laws, our best friends, or sometimes our acquaintances. They may put our temperament to the test by bringing us to the limit of our strength. Each day has its battle. If we think of all the possibilities that we may encounter tomorrow or the day after and in a month or a year, we drive ourselves crazy, unwilling to proceed with the carrying of our cross. Each and every one of us fights our own battles. When a person is the problem of our dismay, we just stop to communing with that individual and the solution is easier and faster. But, what about when we are dealing with an illness, when we are in pain? It is hard enough when a family member is struck with such a thing, especially if that loved one is the provider of our household. It is devastating. What happens when the challenge we have to confront is our own sickness? All the dreams and goals evaporate, and we find ourselves hopeless and in despair. All these are situations we do not consider when we are okay. Wait a second. This does not mean that we are going to live a miserable life thinking of the what-ifs about the future. We do not even know if we will make it through the night to see tomorrow. The same thing is also true for the past. We may spend sleepless nights thinking the same thing, what if we had done or said something different, maybe this, and maybe that. Stop! There has been no human being, and will not be one who can fix the mistakes of the past. Time does not discriminate, and it does not wait for anyone nor brings you to the past to undo, even if you were willing to pay so much for the penalization. The thing is that there is no compensation. If that was the case, anyone, especially the wealthy people would be going back in time more often than you would think, trying to fix their mistakes and shortcomings, but that is impossible. Regarding the future, the same thing prevails. No one knows if we will even wake up tomorrow morning. Our reality and a tangible one, is our today, now. What we are doing with everything assigned to us is what counts. If, and again, here I am with the if, but for the purpose of illustrating the example, here it is: What if all of us, inhabitants of the earth, make the time to discover the beauty of that wonderful house and family members? The thought is incredible, exciting and worthy of winning the Noble Peace Prize around the world. I believe that this planet of ours would be free of all the corruption confronting us in each new situation. The idea is that like in every other career or task in life, we must be creative and experience the moment full of good expectations, wanting to be positive all the time. See the beauty in every person and in every thing around us. Believe in the good intentions of people. Of course, it is our duty to be informed and make the appropriate research when in doubt of someone's advice or affirmation about a matter. In the end, the only person responsible to give an account of your time lived on this earth will be the same one that you see in the mirror. No one else. Sooner or later we will be accountable for each and every thought and action in that regard. Do you agree?"

--Esther, who was among the ones who did not want to even pass by the designated chair, finally requested her turn. We were surprised and happy to hear what she had to share. She began:

Chapter 18

Separation of our Children

"Shattered dreams? I have come to the conclusion that God is merciful and allows us to go through the separation of our children, little by little, one day at a time, so it won't hurt us that much. Imagine if it all happened at once, I am sure we, mothers, would pass out, have a heart attack or something. How is it that those precious newborn were all dependent on their mothers, and after a few years they started dressing themselves? They did not need us as much. As they got older, they continued to be more independent, and their mothers were less important to them. They love us, but someone else came into their lives, and that new person whom they hadn't even known a few months earlier, became the center of their lives. Meaning, that person is more important to them than their mother. That is the law of God. A man will leave his parents to join his wife, and both become one flesh. The clear thing here is that they chose their companion. Many times, we, their mothers, have the sixth sense, that inner voice. The Holy Spirit will tell us that the person who is taking most of our child's time and mind, is not the right choice, for the different reasons that are enumerated one by one. What happens when we tell our children? They begin to be defensive and protective of their other half. Therefore, the mothers become the enemy. How in the world can this be, if we love them with all our being and want the best for them? Well, that is exactly what happens. The in-law notices the friction between our children and us, their mothers. It seems that the person taking their attention takes advantage of the situation and starts taking steps ahead towards the separation of our children from their mother. I do not know the reason for this incomprehensible fact. But, the truth of the matter is that we, the mothers, become the ones giving in to the situation, and asking the in-law to forgive us for something that did not even cross our minds. However, in this case we have to be smart and courageous to fight the good fight. Yes, because if we do not act upon the matter, and immediately, we may end up losing our kids to the in-law. Remember, that is exactly what they want. So, we have to be wise and more intelligent than the person creating those ideas in our children's minds. It can be just saying: "hello," helping with the house or the children. It does not matter. The point here is that we, the mothers, need to be wise, observe a lot and speak as needed, because any situation not well planned, can result in the loss of our children. Remember, it is better to deal with the truth from the very beginning, because later on our children's offspring may arrive, and if we are not on good terms with the now new family of our descendants, we may not only lose our own, but will never enjoy the grandchildren. We, the mothers, not only spent the more needy time with our sons, we cleaned, cooked, washed their dirty clothes, and so many other things. It is not fair that someone from the outside world just shows up one day in our children's lives and moves the heaven and the stars down to earth, just to get them away from us, because they want to have the full control of their lives and wills. That is when we step in, very cautiously, to make sure that whatever we do is genuinely coming from the heart. Because of the way the in-law's actions affect the love of our lives, our children, we must act wiser and smarter. The fruits of our work as mothers, will give up our feelings in order to see our children happy. Shattered dreams? When we give birth to each one of our children, we, mothers, basically put our life at risk in order for that human being to come to life. We offer our life for the new born. Yes, I know, it is the law of life for women to give birth, but at a high cost. It is the same thing. The point that I want to bring to life is this: When a couple, a man and a woman, decide to join their lives to make a home for a family of their own, before the first baby is born, the couple join efforts and goals to make that home a welcoming place for the kids God assigns to their care. Stage by stage of their lives together, raise their kids and the family grows. However, there is a time when one of the members of that loved family wakes up to the calling to start a search for that special someone who is going to be their partner and with whom they will join efforts to form a new family of their own. Well, sometimes it may be the perfect way that all families around the world wish for, but it is hardly ever that it happens that way. In the search for that special someone, there may be an experimental process where the courtship and the parties who are part of the journey, have their minds and bodies submerged in the mud of the world. Prejudice? No, not at all, but it is a reality. When this happens, the family members of the house suffer the consequences of the poor decisions of that family member. That is when we see the shortage of funds, the parents' disagreements, disappointments, and the stress of not being prepared and ready to confront the avalanche of the storm at hand. God is just, and in His word He establishes the consequences of disobedience. Therefore, since whatever acts that are not in accord with the plan of God for that family, punishment will be dealt to the entire household. Usually, the ones who suffer the consequences are the parents, one parent more than the other. That is why we see that the parents are distracted from their tasks and put all their efforts in to trying to save that family member. Usually, the mother is the victim of the cup of God's wrath upon that family. People call it menopause. The experts have even assigned an age when women suffer for an imbalance of the hormones, but is it really that? Have you stopped to think that it is around that time that the first child is experimenting to fly from the nest, and makes a mess? Yes, this is something that the parents or the family expected. The mother, by nature, and because of her assignment, is the one in charge of making sure that everything is used and in order at home. That is her mission. So, when the mess appears in her territory, she does not know what to do, because, according to her, everything with her children is under control. Unfortunately, the parents have not been equipped with a manual on how to act or react to each challenge on the way to the fulfillment of our mission and we take our last breath on this earth. Life is like a puzzle. Every single day we add a small peace to it, until completed. Let's return to the mother and her first child. When her routine is altered for whatever reason, maybe because the pincipal at her child's school calls her to let her know that her precious kid did not go to school, the homework was incomplete, or according to her, her perfect child was in a fight and must be suspended from school, the mother's first reaction is of disbelief. How can this be? There must be a mistake; the fruit of her love is not capable of those things to which the caller was referring. No, there must be a misunderstanding. Imagine what is going on with her hormones. Menopause? Yes, you can say that again.

Shattered dreams? After all is said and done. After we accept the shattered dreams, our bodies go into a purging process. During this time, we feel weak and sensitive. There are some times when we do not even want to get up from our bed. We feel sick. People call this depression? It may be, but it is a normal process that our body, soul and spirit go through when we are letting go of our beloved dream and start accepting the facts of our present reality. It does not matter what our ideal goal was. We are humans and have feelings. Some of us are stronger than others. For some of us, this process may take just a few hours, for some, days, and for some, even years. Also, it has to do with how deep the wound was. Some of us take things more seriously than others. We are unique and different. So, it depends on our uniqueness how we experience different things. Me? Well, I think I have gone through so many situations, that I do not have anything left to feel. That is what I say right now. I feel empty, like I do not care about anything. I just pray for the best for each one of the members of my family first, and then our friends and neighbors, for the peace around the world, specifically for the peace of Jerusalem. I look back when everything started, four years ago. Correction, more than that, maybe seven years ago, but I did not feel it much in the beginning, because I thought it was a temporary thing. As time passed and the adverse circumstances were more and more often, I realized that I just had to hold on. Not only that, it is sad for me to know that I was the pillar of my household. I have always worked, and my husband got used to me bringing the whole check to cover the expenses of our house. I only stayed with my kids on the weekends, holidays and two weeks vacation in a year, and of course, when I was on maternity leave for a month max. My husband got used to me being the provider, whatever he made was 'extra' he thought. Now that I am all worn up and tired, not physically, but emotionally, he has been forced to try to provide to pay the essential necessities; he finds it difficult. Every time I ask to pay for something, he complains. I sadly realize that I can't depend on him on a continual basis, because today he may give gladly, but tomorrow he may be complaining. I opted not to ask him anymore, but then, if I don't do that, I may end up without phone service, etc. Even though he may work to bring the money, that is all he does; he does not know what bill needs to be paid. If I left it up to him, I am wondering where we would be by now. By trying to keep the essentials going, I have to remind him every day of our responsibilities, and we get into disagreements because he complains that I am asking too much for money. When we had the means to pay for everything and more, he did not pay the bills; imagine now that he has to work, the bills can wait according to him. Every decision we have made lately is depending on him who tries to avoid his responsibilities. But, what happens with me? I do not have the drive to find a job or get myself busy working my way out of this situation. I am walking with sadness and disappointment in my heart, knowing that everyone, including my husband, is depending on me to do something about it; borrowing money or making arrangements. The way I feel is that he knows that I am going to do something, as I have always done. So, why worry about anything?

Shattered dreams? Maybe you are attracting that, some may say. Really? No. I do not think so. Is it the consequence of some bad actions in the past that you are now reaping what you sowed? All these are factual good questions and possibilities, but what is really going on, and why? Well, it is very simple. It is the process of growing up and changing stages in life. That is why we started our sharing by asking: Who does not have shattered dreams? We all know for sure that we can all relate with this scenario. It is as if we shed our skin every time we go through an experience where our dreams are shattered. It does not matter how high we are, when we go through the process of being molded to the image of God, we must come down from our pedestals, When we hit rock bottom, there is a certain stigma with which the human race identifies. We adjust and settle to continue the journey, then we encounter another change and we sink even lower. There are some of us, who through the commotion of the changes and rebirthing, feel that we are at the bottom of the pit. It may be the truth, let me tell you, because there are some times that we have to hit the very bottom to accept the facts of life. Some of us live our lives complaining and whining about something that we cannot change. Every day people's dreams are shattered and spirits broken. Instead of resisting the truth, it is a matter of embracing the change and adjusting to a new beginning. I am sure that there are people who in their life span on this earth go through several changes, some more than other. Some just a few, but those few counted for all the rest that the more experienced in the subject have gone through. Our country has gone to a tremendous effort for us to have peace and pretend that everything is okay. That is why we are provided with all kind of services, so we do not recognize our shattered dreams. The fact is that we have everything handed to us, we buy things that sometimes we do not use, all these in an effort to fill the void of that shattered dream. However, there is no escape from this inevitable passing through sooner or later. It is not if, but when. We go to the malls to buy and get more in debt, trying to fill that missing essence of our being. We try to avoid the tears and the crushing of our ego or disappointment, but guess what? Whether we like it or not, we must go through the fire to be refined like gold. So, why prolong the wait or the pain of facing reality to be a better human being? Everything is a matter of accepting reality just the way it is. There is no such thing as white and black, some say. We prefer the gray line. But, guess what? Sooner or later we are going to come out of that area to face the punishment of deterring the inevitable. As we are taken away from that comfort zone and placed in an area that is not appealing nor to our comfort, we start resenting or blaming whoever and whatever we may think is responsible for our misfortune. But, when we just accept the things as they pass by us or as they are, we will be delivered from the anguishing pain that we feel so intently, and we will be amazed. God is good, and does not allow us to miss our target in life. We may be going through the thorns right now, but please, do not forget this: the light at the end of the tunnel can be seen by everyone. When we go through the darkest moments in our life, the good thing to do is to read the Bible and take a nap, because when people do not sleep well, they are cranky and very negative. We must look at the good side of things in every area of our lives. When things are not going our way could we call this shattered dreams? Well, we could, because we were heading towards one direction and different circumstances are taking us to an absolutely dissimilar path. However, there is a reason for everything, and it usually is for our own good, even though at that particular moment we do not understand it. When all the pieces of our life get put together and we are able to see the whole picture, then we will be assured and grateful of all the things we went through. At least that is what I think and hope for."

--Rebecca stands up and starts walking towards the appointed chair. She doesn't even care how cold her coffee is, she sips it a little, and then she says:

Chapter 19

The Surprising Will

"There is this story that comes to mind right now, and I think it goes with what I am trying to express on this subject. There was a realtor, who probably was not doing well on her sales, or was having problems with her family, or maybe was, according to her, punishing herself for something from her past that was tormenting her. In order to be at peace with her conscience, or to believe that she was paying back somehow, she decided to visit the homeless at a park and bring lunch to each and every one of them there. This was not done every day, but every other day or so. As she was doing that, she was feeling good about herself because she was obeying her heart. She was doing it smiling and not making distinctions. She talked to them and helped them as she could. The homeless there knew her and were expecting her the days she brought them lunch. One day, a new member of that group came unexpected; the realtor was short on her orders for that hour. However, she did not say anything nor was she surprised. The new member was the last one to be served. She gave him her lunch. He noticed that, because she sat next to him, but did not eat. This man admired the good deed of this lady who was taking the funds and the time to be among those men and women in need at that park. This lady's routine continued for days, months and years. One day, the man who had eaten this lady's lunch the first time he had joined the group there, was sick, and the police took him to a hospital. When the lady found out what had happened, she made arrangements to visit him at the hospital. By this time, she knew them by name. So, imagine the smile she brought to this old man when she showed up to see him. It happened that he did not survive the surgery, and he died. Time passed, I am talking about months. One day, the realtor received notice that she needed to be present at the reading of a homeless old man's will. Of course, she was surprised. How was it that the homeless old man could have a will? Surely this was a mistake, she thought. She read and read the notification in disbelief, but she showed up at the appointed place and time. To her surprise, there were many different elegant people that she had never seen before in her life. They all looked at her, as if asking: "Who is this lady?" They asked the attorney if that was a mistake, but to their amazement, they could not start the reading of the will until she arrived. The realtor lady did not imagine why she was called to attend the meeting. But, guess what? The homeless old man, actually, he was not that old anyway. The attorney started reading the old man's wishes. The cars, the houses, and other belongings were divided among the members of the family present, but the millions of dollars in different accounts were to be given to his realtor friend who had genuinely cared for him. He did not have to share the benches at that park with the rest of the homeless there, but he was tired of his family members who were after his money. He disappeared and decided to be homeless. There is where he made up his mind to leave his fortune to this lady who had cared for the less fortunate. Therefore, that money of his could not be left in better hands, because she would know how to distribute it fairly and wisely to be a blessing to others. Can you believe this? The realtor followed the calling of her heart to do well unto others, and she was blessed through one of the same members of that community that she had served. Being genuine and caring for others pay back with interest. Don't you agree?

Shattered dreams? I say that there are different ways of expressing what we feel when we experience that reverse in our lives. Each movie or TV show is based on a true story, but by adding names and details to it, the movie falls into the fiction category. The main thing about all these different experiences, or the purpose of all these is to detect on time when the dream is being shattered for whatever reason, and find the ways to stop the shattering or to be mentally prepared not to suffer as much as when all of a sudden the dream is broken all the way. That is when it hits us altogether and takes us more time to recuperate from the impact, and we do not have the strength or courage to pick up the pieces to start weaving a new dream. There are times when a dream is shattered, the pieces were picked up and a new dream was begun. Again, that second dream went through the same shattering as the original dream. The pieces get picked up. But to create a new dream is more painful. Sometimes it is just impossible to do anything with those small pieces; they end up in the waste. The emptiness of that void left takes time to heal. But, when that hope makes a way to fill that vacant space, a brand new dream arises, and there are some times that this new dream becomes a bigger and better one. There are so many different stories from so many people around the world. Which one is yours? In this, there could be the seed of a new book, movie or TV show. Do you see what I am saying when I tell you that there is a real story behind those great creations brought to the big screen? The dreams that were shattered and went through the process of healing, and trying again and again, are the ones that are worthy of telling to show others and give them hope to keep trying, and to never give up. If others before us could do it, we can do it also. The motto behind each and every circumstance or situation is a key factor to determine how long the process will take to heal. There are two groups. The genuine ones, and the fake ones used to control and manipulate. These are not dreams, but nightmares, forced to exist to damage or shatter someone else's. The real ones are those that are based on love and caring for others from conception. Those are the ones with which the whole universe cooperates, and makes the way for things and people to get together for the purpose of bringing to life that beautiful and genuine dream. God is a Creator. Therefore, we by nature have that gift in us. That is why, while we are doing something in the physical realm, in our minds we are creating or weaving a completely different and new creation. Daydreaming, some call it. That is the beauty that differentiates us from the rest of the inhabitants of the earth. We, the human beings, are creative and creators of those dreams. Some of them may come to life in perfect and timely manner, but I warn you; there is not even one that has not had a war going in order to come to its realization. Sometimes we give up at the edge of touching the reality of our dreams. Why is this? Well, different factors, but reason number one to consider is that we give up and do not allow the cycle to complete, so we can move towards a new stage or page in our life. I am sorry to say this, but many of us do not educate ourselves to hold on until we have the specific and correct instruction from God, our inside, to do so. When we move sooner or later to accomplish our dreams, they will not come to pass, because we have to be educated on the rules and regulations of the Creator of the dreams.

Shattered dreams? There are times when our age is not to our favor. Our energy is not helping us to accomplish our dreams. Our minds are the same as when we were young, but our bodies do not move the same. We feel tired and do not have the same expectations in life; we are worn out, and want our own space to relax and just be ourselves. There is a time and a season for every single thing under the sun. The stages of our lives lined up by the Creator are unique and specific for the purpose and timing designed for the occasion. When our children are young, we have to be on the run most of the time, taking care of them; our energy levels are very high because we need that. But, when we advance in time, and our children grow up, they start helping with the chores in the house. The main thing is that they clean after themselves and start being equipped to fly and make lives of their own. We are left behind with the memories and the regrets of the things that we could have done better. So, it may take us time to get over those regrets and keep living. It is okay to feel tired and sad some times. It is part of our existence on this earth. We all get over everything. If we could just realize that when we had that beautiful house and the different furniture, it was because our children needed all that while they lived with us. Therefore, we all needed those commodities to live happily and to enjoy each other as best as we could. The time spent looking back and wishing to change the things already done; please excuse me, but it is an infliction of pain that is unnecessary, because the truth is that we cannot change anything. What happened is that what we lived was meant for that specific time and season of our lives, and it was good, very good! Instead, when we start feeling down and depressed about those memories, we must be humbled and ask God for His merciful forgiveness. The most important process is to forgive ourselves, because that is the thorn in our flesh that will torment us for the rest of our lives if we do not learn to forgive ourselves. Just remember that we, all human beings on earth, go through the same things. Except that some are able to wake up earlier than others to the realization of accepting themselves and keep going with the new goals and building of those new dreams. Maybe to surprise the grandchildren at their graduation, or go to those places that we wanted to visit, but that for whatever reason we kept postponing and procrastinating. There are so many things we can do with our free time now. As we know, life is unique and worth living to the fullest. We are just the parents for a season in our children's lives. Do not take things so much to heart. They are not worth it, especially if thinking about them hurt us. Please, do not get me wrong. If a purging and cleansing is required to refresh our inner soul, blessed be the process and the time invested in it, because it must happen in order to keep going and make peace with ourselves. I am so happy that we are sharing what we think. Now I leave the famous chair to whoever wants to be next"

--This time Manuela and Kate got up at the same time to share their stories, but Kate decided to let Manuela go first. Manuela accepted the honor. She sat comfortably and said:

Chapter 20

Relatives and Friends

Yes. It is hard to believe that all the friends and relatives we used to entertain and travel with are there, but are not available when we need them the most. Well, there may be different factors. Some of them see you as you were before, meaning, that they may not know the downward spiral your life took and that you are in need now, or they may have an idea and are embarrassed to ask you straight if you need help. Who knows what happens, but the truth of the matter is that everywhere you go, you feel bad. Why? Because you know what is bothering you, and you are among the people who "supposedly" care and love you. You wish they would ask you if you are in need and offer you their help. Instead, they ignore your situation, and you feel worse than when you arrived to visit them. What is going on? The problem is that we sometimes do not know how to read the body language of our neighbors. The most common answer to this is that we do not care enough to see the slumped shoulders, the fake smile, etc. When we care about someone, we immediately can tell when that loved one cried, the contradictions of the story told, or even how the person behaves. There are many ways that people in need cry for help, but for obvious reasons, embarrassment and shyness, that person cannot express the request of his or her soul, which is: please, help me! There are sometimes when we can apply the saying in the Bible that avers: do not let your right hand know what your left hand does. In other words, help your neighbors without them asking, especially when you know that this person is in need, and you can help. There are so many opportunities God puts in our way to help others, but we decide to ignore, so our soul reproaches us at night when we are alone and quiet. I challenge you to pay attention to your relatives or friends when they call or visit you. There is always a reason for a person to move towards your direction. So, what is the motive for that visit or call? Check the body language of your visitor. When you check the body language or the tone of voice of the person on the other end of the phone, please remember. What is my assignment out of this conversation? When you do that, your journey through this earth will be complete, and the job for that particular day accomplished. When we do not even let the visitor or caller say what the need is because we felt it, and we basically provided the answer or offered the help, the other person's gratitude is going to be a heartfelt one, not a forced one. Genuinely loving your neighbor as yourself is the key to everything we do. This is the Golden Rule God wants us to follow. In the ladder of experience per se, we get to take our turn to get to this point. First, our parents help us, even before we ask for anything. They know what we need, and they provide it all. Do you remember? Later, we ask, and they provide. There is a time when we are the providers, and that is the time of stepping up in the ladder of accomplishment and success - the time when we freely give. People say that it is better to give than to receive. Well, that is exactly what we do when we meet others' needs. As you already know, not many people come to you. The only people who call you and knock at your door are the God-sent ones whom He wants you to help, or be helped by on your journey to the real and fulfilled life in heaven.

Shattered dreams? Many times. But as they say, this is the way of life while in this physical body on this earth. Everywhere we go, every person we meet, as we listen to their stories, there is always a shattered dream or broken spirit somewhere.

For instance, when everything seems to be running as planned, all of a sudden, something happens that brings us to that crossroad where we start doubting, get confused, and start making the wrong decisions. We then come back to that common ground of confusion and disappointment. Even though we have been in that same arena many times, these last years before crossing the hill and arriving at that golden age of our lives, make us a more vulnerable and easy target to so many different downfalls. Every so often we encounter those crossroads. It is not a matter of if, but when we are going to be confronting those tough decisions in our lives. There are those times when all those ideas and goals were so reachable, that we thought we could touch them with our fingertips. But, for one reason or another, we just have to take a break or put them to rest for a little bit. Maybe they flew away because they were the result of that emotional stage we were in when confronted with that bump or crossroad in our journey. I do not know if you can relate to me when I share this with you: The feeling of being empty, no dreams, no ambition; just the here and now moment. I have been thinking about this sensation of nothing but pure existence. Have you heard about the sabbatical year? Could it be that? Maybe there is that time in our lives when we have that urge of solitude and the need to rest, that time when our bodies command us to let go and relax. Even if you put yourself to the task of being busy and working towards some part of that goal that you initially set for yourself, your mind is not there with you. Your body may be there, but it is empty, because the energy required to create those things to get to the desired accomplishment is not there. Then, I ask. What is the point of appearing to be busy doing something, when in reality nothing is being accomplished? It is much better to wait and have everything that is required to obtain the results of the hard and enjoyable work of doing what it takes to get to the top of the hill. There are times when we are crossing that strange field. Not many people talk about the real things they experience and go through. For some reason, we all pretend to have it all together, and if someone is candid enough to express in words what is really going on inside of himself or herself, those that pretend to have the world under their control tag him or her as out of this planet, mentally disabled or incompetent of taking care of himself or herself. Every one of us is trying to be better than our neighbors. Our world and our lives could be so different and for the better if we were genuine, and if elders were honest in sharing their experiences and telling us what would they have done differently in order to help the young to get to the top of that hill in one piece at a faster pace. Many of us die on the journey and never make it to the destination, because at the fork in the road, we take the wrong turn and end up in the pit of destruction. Some of us did not move from the safe spot that we thought we were in. Therefore, we did not have the courage to make the move that our hearts were sometimes pushing us to make, we hesitated and decided to stay still in the same place, condemning our offspring to grow roots in the same polluted land. It is amazing to see people with incredible talents, who because of the territory they grew up, used those talents for the wrong causes, or simply slowly died with no hope of developing their full potential. Our decisions are very important. They do not only affect the outcome of our own lives, but of those of our generation. As I said before, we need to open up and be honest with ourselves first, and then with others. Hopefully we can help at least one person to make a difference, to stand up among the crowd, and be the great man or woman God intended for each one to be.

It is with sadness that I report to you that I tried to open up, and be honest with myself and with my fellow men. But, instead of the person I was sharing my ideals with being receptive, and on the same page of freedom and accomplishment, this person opted to take advantage of my honesty and tried to abuse the trust I expressed. So, there is not only that group of superiority among us, but that other of lions dressed in sheep's clothing. No wonder Jesus warned us of that group, and gave us the instruction of being wise as a serpent and gentle as a dove. Why? So we could not show at first sight our true colors to the enemy. We need to be wise and try the spirits around us. Because not everyone is who they say they are. We will know them by their fruits. For out of the abundance of the heart the mouth speaks. There is only one concept that will never fail: We are not responsible for others' behavior, but our own. Therefore, anywhere we are, wherever we go, let us be ourselves; the incredible and distinctive beings that we were created to be. We are different, but at the same time unique and one in God. How can we all being part of that great, omnipotent and omnipresent God, try to destroy each other instead of helping each one to be the best that each and every one of us can be? We are in a classroom at home with our mate and our children. There, we can put into practice all the lessons of life in our hearts. We are creative by nature. We have so many different opportunities to redeem ourselves and create wonderful things in our household. After a certain age or stage in our life, God gives us the opportunity to rediscover ourselves with those new talents refined by the knowledge accumulated through the years of experience in practicing every single day with our own at home. Once we are ready for the next journey, we can share with others until we graduate from the best school, our own life. On graduation night or our funeral, people will honor us with their presence. They will be sharing how we touched their lives. Some may share what we did for them at a young age, some at midway through, and some towards the end. The point is that each and every one there present have something to say about us. There are going to be people that our immediate family do not know. Even they will be surprised to know from those strangers things about us that they did not give themselves the time to discover, and maybe by the fact that others will be sharing the same things we tried to emphasize so many times in different ways while with them and did not get it. It would be at that time by paying attention to those same words in the lips and the voice of third parties that they will finally get it deep in their souls, and will share it with their children and their grandchildren. Do you see the importance of touching lives along the way of our journey through this earth? Do not be discouraged, and do not dismay about the intent to change our world and our family for the best. Sooner or later those plants will fructify. It is possible that we may not see it with our physical eyes and will not enjoy the fruits, but the main point is that because of that small or even great something we did, created that change in that beautiful life. No one is an accident or a waste. We are all-important and are here specifically chosen and for a purpose. We are all created equal, and at the same time different, but again, for a purpose. In one's life there are so many people's touch involved. Just think. There were two required to procreate that one life. Then came along the grandparents on both sides, now there are six people, not counting the uncles and aunts from both parties, the brothers and sisters, the cousins, the friends of each one of them, the babysitters, etc. But, shattered dreams? It does not matter what we have gone through in our short or long life. Time is a process that we all experience and have to go through, like it or not. That is an inevitable road that we all have to walk. Our core, the essence of our very being is strong, brave, a conqueror, a victorious winner. That is the reason we do not readily accept defeat. We were made to find the ways out of each and every adverse situation. Sometimes we spend extra time trying to fix and revive the dead from the grave. This could be situations we face in our day to day living, as well as people in our immediate family and sphere of influence. It is understandable. We are human and relate to one another. We do not want to leave anyone or anything without giving them the benefit of the doubt and a second chance. But, unfortunately, there are times when there is nothing else we can do but walk. I completely agree that we all want to have that peace of mind when and if we encounter the same situation or people again on our paths. We want to be able to look and walk straight with no regrets. So, it does not matter how much time we spent in our past endeavors. As we grow in experience and maturity, we realize that we do not have much time to waste. Yes, let us call things by their name and by what they are. Even though we know that everything works together for good to those who want to be in the perfect center of God's will, let us not abuse or tempt God. With time we become wiser and have better discernment to say, yes or no to whatever we encounter in our journey through this planet called Earth. Every circumstance that we face in our life is people related. Therefore, we are going to address the following with society. It does not matter how the subject is presented, the bottom line to consider is whether or not it is honoring and empowering others. Life is a win-win situation. Every time we realize this result, we can be assured that we are making the right decision, and we can bet on that person bringing the problem or situation at the stage of judgment for support. That is how we distinguish the just and brave people who have the heart of God in themselves. They are the ones on whom we can lean with our eyes closed because they will never fail us. Everything they do is thinking as if they are doing it to themselves. These kind of people are trustworthy. Of course, in this imperfect world it is difficult to find them, but believe me, they exist and are a blessing to whoever finds them in their midst. Sometimes they are in the body of an old being to whom no one pays attention, because they think that an old person is a burden to the close family and to society in general. Is it not strange and an irony that society and science are in the goal of experimenting euthanasia with them? They say that these old members of society are an expense, and the young generations need more funds. I am not saying that all the gray-haired people have the same golden seed in them. Not at all. By their fruits we will know them. I am talking about the genuine, wise, experienced and well-intentioned people, who work hard. Hard? Yes, they work hard on their knees, in the middle of the night, praying for you and me, so that we may have a better world in which to live. These elderly people do not sleep much. Some of them have dreams and visions, and know much better than the regular people around them. Remember that they are seldom listened to. Yes, because sometimes they do not smell well, they do not see with their physical eyes; meaning that they are blind and need help. We avoid them because they imply time and work from us. It is a shame that sometimes we do not even take care of our own elderly people. We take them to nursing homes. I can understand when we do this because of illness or the circumstances around us, by doctor's prescriptions, or even by us being incapable of taking care of them. But, just because our elderly are a burden to us and we do not find the leisure to go parties etc.? Let us meditate a little bit. There is a saying about an elderly that goes like this: As you see yourself, I once saw myself; as you see me now, you will be seen one day. We have to be careful. As we treat others, we may end up being treated ourselves."

--Manuela stopped and kept silent for a few minutes. Kate got up and approached Manuela, who was like daydreaming. Kate had to poke her in the shoulder to request the chair. Everyone in the kitchen kept quiet and anxious to hear what Kate had to say. Kate looked at each one of us there, and said:

Chapter 21

Elderly People

Talking about elderly people. Many times we encounter people that because of their gray hair and golden-year appearance, we want to trust. Yes, they are so close to crossing the bridge of return towards the eternal destination, that we would not think they were taking revenge at whatever cost for their shattered dreams of the past. The sad side of this situation is that they do not care who, according to them, will pay the consequences of their misfortunes. Here may come this poor woman who is having disagreements in her marriage, so she thinks that this old lady would be able to give her a good advice from her previous experience in life. What a disappointment. This old lady is very experienced in how she seduces and controls people's minds. In this case, she twists the information received and puts in her victim's mind the big picture of what she wants the young woman to see. Kind of what happened in the Garden of Eden with the serpent and Eve. The young woman is convinced of what the old lady planted in her mind. The marriage of this innocent woman is going to be destroyed. Guess what? The old lady's marriage was destroyed, and because she has not been able to settle this disappointment in her life and is not at peace; instead of not wanting those young women around her passing through the same valley she went through, she hates each one of them that has a blessed marriage, and she is jealous of the happiness she sees in others. Therefore, her venomous sting destroys whoever gets close to her. That is why is so important not to go with the first and only opinion of someone. We see people, but we do not really know their intentions. In this particular case, the young woman wanted to leave her husband because she was going out with her husband's best friend. She wanted someone who would back her intentions, and she found the perfect one. But, when you are genuinely looking for an answer to your doubts, and approach that elderly person for the best advice that you could ever receive, be careful. By their fruits, you will know them. Even though they may be dressed in sheep's clothing, they are furious lions finding someone innocent to devour. Be careful. Run from those kind of people. What you want and see in the spirit is exactly what you will get. These same patterns apply to good and bad. That is why we have to be careful when we make up our minds. Sometimes we may regret it later, because we may be condemning innocent people to leave the house never to come back. The spouse can react and opt to not allow them to return. It is wiser and best to get a second opinion, or consult with a professional. Just remember, they are not God and have their own problems like you and I, and some times they have bigger problems than you and I. Don't forget, they are human, and it does not matter how many titles are hanging on that wall; they make mistakes. People work in different positions and we use their services, but the last word is said and done by the most interested party, you, the only one affected by the circumstances. Let us be wise and do not let anyone fool us. There are only two sides to everything in life, good and evil. I pray that every time you are confronted with a challenge that you think has a way out, you can find a way to share with others whatever you have learned in the process to your success story-telling. Even though we tried to cover up for you in this arena, you have a decision to make and must be willing to pay the cost for that happiness. Nothing is for free in this life. I am sorry, but if you are getting everything for free, without pain as cost for whatever you need, you are missing out, because one day the accrued interest will be added to your account.

Shattered dreams? Have you thought about our journey through this Earth? We all have to go through the same roads and bridges. When we first arrive into this world, we cross the bridge that we will call "The Tunnel Bridge." We make that triumphant entrance. Our mother's arms are anxious and stretched out to welcome us and to introduce us to our father, then our brothers and sisters, our grandmothers, our grandparents, and then to the rest of the family and friends. Our mother is the guide, our guardian angel, who shows us everything there is to learn for our survival. She loves us and has the best interest in our accomplishments in this life. Our father is there also. He provides all the economic means for our existence, but we spend most of the time with our mother in this place that is called "Toddlerhood." In this town we have plenty of time to play and sleep. All our needs are taken care of by others, meaning our parents and the members in our household. As we grow up and are able to take care of our own main necessities, we will now cross the bridge that is called "Childhood." We do the crossing by the hands of our parents. We spend time in that town that is named after the same name of the bridge. While we are there, we make friends, we play, attend school, and meet new people outside of our family circle. We are in the process of learning to relate to other human beings like us. We start to see the world we live in through the eyes of the teacher and the books. Once in a while we witness disagreements between the other children while they play, occasionally we observe and even participate in a fight. Sometimes we do not want to go back to school because we are afraid. In our short time on this earth, we start exploring feelings that are new to us. Our parents resolve all of our problems. They know everything, and of course, we do not worry about anything; our parents fix whatever conflict we may have with our friends or at school. We experience our first graduation, which is from kindergarten; then we go to elementary school. There, we are among more students, and we are now exposed to a wider environment. We are learning to behave and respect others, because in that bigger school, there are older kids. Sometimes we want to be like them, or we may even be afraid of them. Graduation comes from that place, now we are going to move to another school, sometimes we do not have to move, but we will only change classrooms, now we are older and will be attending middle school. We will experience new responsibilities, maybe more homework. Our experience in life is growing, and our tasks are more, but our parents are still responsible for everything we need. We just go to school, enjoy our friends, play and help with some chores assigned to us at home. By this time, when we moved to middle school, we are also going to start crossing that bridge that is called "Teenagerhood." Our parents have been holding our hands and they must continue doing so, because this is one of the most critical bridges we are going to cross while in this physical body and our journey in this temporary life. But, we do not want to hold our parents' hand; we want to cross it alone. They can only be at a distance watching us. We understand that we need them because we are afraid, but at the same time, we want them as far away as possible. We do not want our friends to be talking or laughing saying that we are immature, that we still need our parents. We think that we are older. In fact, we think we know more than our parents; they are so behind in technology and fashion. We know better at this age. So, we start crossing the bridge. Our parents love us. Sometimes they respect our wishes by being behind us at a distance, but sometimes, they do not care what we say and are going to be holding our hands, like it or not. It depends on what the personality and character of our parents are. This bridge is about seven years long, dark and shaky. I told you; it is the most dangerous of all the bridges we must cross. We graduate from middle school, and now we are going to change schools; we are attending high school. We will meet new people, make new friends, our responsibilities increase, and our bodies are also in a beautiful and better shape than when we started in 6th grade. We feel that we have the whole world beneath our feet. We want to act and behave like grown-ups, like our parents and other adults around us. But guess what? We still are under our parent's guidance. Our parents are just behind us to make sure that we can safely cross that bridge of teenage-hood. This is the most dangerous bridge. Since we think that we are grown-ups and know it all, it is so easy to fall. The problem is that if we fall, we are going to harm ourselves so badly that we will never be the same again. As we are crossing this dangerous bridge under our parents' care, we are whole, but once we make a false move and fall, we will never be whole again, we will have to pick up the pieces left on our fall and recreate ourselves. There is no need for this. Why mend while this fall can be avoided? Unfortunately, there are so many of us that are falling or have fallen from this bridge, that only a handful of people make it to the other side unharmed. Why? I can say that it is because of knowledge and understanding. We just let go by what our eyes see. We do not slow down to meditate and consider the consequences of our actions. We think that our parents do not know anything. Sometimes it is true, because our parents for lack of knowledge push us off the bridge themselves. Yes. It sounds incredible, but that is the truth. Seldom we know of those who at that young age experienced the fall from the bridge that we cross entering the middle school years;

their lives are destroyed. Imagine how careless those parents were, that they let their precious ones fall... What we experienced while crossing the bridges is what we will bring in our toolbox for our children. Therefore, if our parents themselves fell off from this dangerous bridge back in their own time, they will not be able to discern where the next trap will be, because they did not make it safely to the other side. So, basically, we both are discovering the surprises of the bridge together, with us crossing for the very first and unique time. Remember, even though we wished we could go back in time to do things differently, we just cannot. This is our only time crossing this bridge. I strongly suggest that you be very careful and pay attention to your next step on the crossing of this bridge. Learn and pass with honors this experience, so you can show your own when the time comes for them to do the same thing. But you will be better equipped to help them and bring them unharmed to the other side. Do you see how many of us experience the shattering of our dreams at this early age? Some of us may cross this bridge with ease, because our parents did it, and they are equipped to help us. But, there are some of us that we will not have the same luck for different reasons. Some because our parents failed to do it, and they are guiding us with less than 100% success, some of us because of our parents' ignorance; they throw us off the bridge, and some of us, because we do not pay attention to the loving advice our parents are giving us, and we think that we know it all. This is the saddest scenario, because it may be that our parents successfully crossed this bridge, and of course, they know the tricks and the how to do it. We may have all the potential and possibility of helping our generation to come to do the same, but we are stubborn, arrogant and too proud to accept advice. We may just pretend to know it all, and do it, but because we are not giving 100% of our attention and do not have the conviction of what and why we are doing what we are doing, we are the easy target of defeat to smash our dreams into pieces. It does not matter if God Himself came down from heaven to show us the way to make it safely to the other side, we are so obstinate, haughty and egotistical, that we do not care if we make it in one piece, or in many different little pieces to the other side of the bridge. We will spend a few years in this town that it is called "Adulthood." There, we will graduate from university, we will meet new people in the place of work, or the different places where our presence will be required. We will meet the love of our life, we will go through the courtship process, and get married. Within that same town, "Adulthood," there will be small bridges. One is when we finally leave our parents' house to get married. That bridge, even though some people describe it as the one bridge that no one wants to cross, it is fun when we have the most important person in the universe at that time; our companion for life. That bridge-crossing is the most exciting and happy of our lives. There we live our married life. From here on we are no longer alone, we have our companion, then the children come, we train them and guide them through the same cycle we went through until God calls us back home. There is so much to share in this regard, but I better let the next person continue."

--Kate left the chair, and Gloria took her place. This time the women brought more chairs to the table, as some of us moved to make room for the new members to our group. When everyone was set and ready, Kate nodded to the group and turned to Gloria to commence with her story, and so she did:

Chapter 22

Couples

It doesn't matter if we go back to our childhood or whatever age we are in, the goals and dreams we create need to be fulfilled in order for us to feel alive. This gives us stamina to continue dreaming. Life per se is a dream. We cannot stop dreaming and setting goals. It does not matter how small or how big, a dream at last.

We have dreams that we set as individuals, but when the dream relates to the couple, it is very important to make sure that the word or promise given to the other must be kept in the order established by both of them. If the parties do not get aligned and in order, the goal will not be accomplished, and the trust in each other will be lost. When that happens, the proverb applies where it says: Can two walk together when they are not in agreement? Not at all. The un-kept promises or the half-done tasks affects the desire and the willing of the committed party. One thing entangles the other to the point of disbelief, and the irremediable consequence of the lack of commitment and respect towards the other is the divorce. This is so common in our days that we have not considered the reasons for the couple to proceed to take this drastic recourse. We always assume or think that the reason for someone to request the divorce is because of infidelity, but as you can see, there are many other reasons which are more at heart, and the real consequence may be the irresponsibility and laziness of either party. Have you stopped to think, why this happens in a marriage that both parties were so in love with each other when they got married? It is a process. Each party is willing at that time to give one hundred percent to make their marriage work. The dream was until death set them apart. Then, what happened? Everything has a beginning. Love is the only feeling that is eternal. It does not have an end. Then, do couples fall in love and out of love? The word love in the dictionary has a meaningful interpretation. In the Bible it has a more thoroughly explained significance. There are different meanings and components. The very first moment one of these ingredients fails, and it is not fixed or corrected the same day before the sun goes down; the chain of events afterwards will affect the rest of the ingredients which will start to deteriorate, and the effect of that first consequence not attended will bring the couple to the cross of the two roads, and force them to make that drastic decision. The shattering of dreams is the result of the one or others' failure, for whatever reason, to not perform as expected in the previous agreement or commitment. It does not matter how we try to explain the situation, the bottom line is what it is; lack of respect towards our neighbor. In this case to our close and loved ones.

Shattered dreams? Every time. While we are in this body of flesh and bones on this earth, we were, we are, and we will always be exposed to having our dreams and goals being shattered. Nothing comes to us on a cloud. We have to learn to live with the fact that we are exposed to those kinds of viruses in our environment. The point of our sharing is to help us be aware and prepared for those adverse events, and know what to do. Meaning? Not to let ourselves be broken but to learn to manage the time and moment to re-establish our soul and spirit to bring something new to live. Sometimes we will be amazed at the marvelous things that came up out of that tragedy or destruction of what was being built. Always to keep in mind that everything works together for our own good. It is understandable that we do not want to experiment or move away from our comfort zone, but if you think about it, it is for the best; for others and ourselves. We are not alone, and we can never think of ourselves alone. Please, do not get me wrong. There are times that we have our own moments, when we are within ourselves, those relaxing baths, the time when we get up and take care of our own selves; the same we do in the evening, and why not, in the middle of the day or the afternoon. But, most of the time we are committed to help others.

It is so important to meditate and be alone within ourselves to know the way and the how to do things. It is not important to act as if we are busy doing something, but we need to actually accomplish a goal or task assigned for that particular day. Some of us are just starting to raise a family, some are adjusting to the empty nest stage of our lives. The tasks at hand are different, but each one is important and demanding. Therefore, it does not matter the age, or the stage; what matters is that all among us are related, and the consequences of our decisions and our actions will affect our neighbor one way or the other. As long as we take the responsibility to do the best of our ability to accomplish our assignment at hand, everyone will be okay. Let us put our heart into everything we do, always being conscious that whatever we do is not to or for men, but to and for God. When we are aware and conscious of this truth, our loved ones, our circle of influence, the whole world will be better taken care of. Look at the bakery on the corner. All the employees there are connected and working towards the same goal; serving the public. By doing that, each one of them get paid and are able to provide for their families. The owners do the same thing. We are all around to do the same in the area we serve. The result of all our efforts is to serve the public. Some of us may just be dealing with one person, maybe is the baby assigned to our care, because we babysit for the young mother, or maybe we take care of three or four babies. It does not matter. The point I am trying to make is that everything forms a circle. What I do will carry my mission to the other, who is following my same steps and will continue the project to the next generation, and that next generation to the next, and so forth. Observe the people and their professions around you. Aren't they doing different things, but working towards the same goal? Yes, the result of each one of our efforts is to benefit one or many people. We serve each other, some doing it as a charity, and some doing it for a paycheck or commission. By doing what we are meant to do, we benefit all. Sometimes we believe that only the priests, pastors, and the charity workers are called to serve the neighbor as the Golden Rule commands, but God created us in His image. This might confuse us. So, let us not whine and complain at work too much, etc., let us all be happy and excited at the task assigned to us, because our hands and minds are busy creating and doing something to benefit someone who needs us. All our efforts and minds unite like a prayer that is elevated to heaven, and when this is done in the knowledge that we are giving the best of ourselves, the result and the fruit of our hands elevate in a straight pleasing fragrance of offering to our Creator in a beautiful and accepted praise of gratitude and adoration to Him, who thought of us even before everything was created to be at this place and for this purpose. Shattered dreams? So what? What matters is the result of our shattering, which is the beginning and the opportunity of sharing with others, so they can be better until the best outcome is presented one day in the eternal heavenly places. Let us all focus on the joy and happiness we will have when everything is said and done. When we all are given the opportunity to look back at the work done by us. At that moment, all those shed tears and hurts will not matter, because the excitement of the glorious reward of seeing what was accomplished, without even us knowing it until that particular moment, will compensate everything. We will be shouting for joy. No wonder the Bible tells us to be anxious for nothing, because everything we go through in life is for the best to come. Are we dreamers? You bet we are! But, again, we come to the same thing; we were created this way for a reason and a purpose. Therefore, let us never give up. We fall, let us get up. It does not matter how long it takes us to do it, but let us never stay down. Remember. We are like the eagles that renew their strength, like the palm trees being beaten by the rain and the wind; we may bend, but we don't break. We have been equipped to be conquerors. Every tear shed, every pain suffered, every disappointment, every shattered dream is just a step closer to our glorious crown waiting for us. I just cannot wait to see the fruits of your hands and mine in the real magnitude and meaning assigned to you and me on this earth. Wooh! What a blessing!"

--Gloria started clapping her hands as she got up, and we all joined her in excitement. On the way back to her seat, she pointed at Michelle, who got up and went to sit in the privileged spot. She said:

Chapter 23

Struggles and Stumblings

"What an honor! I will try to share my thoughts, but I think that all of you have already said it all. God in his merciful ways allows elements to align to make people meet along our paths. Sometimes to encourage us and give us hope, other times for us to enlighten their dark moments. We are connected. My experiences may resound in your spirit, or yours may do the same within mine. In this area, the time and the distance are not altering factors. A mother may have been deserted by her husband and her children for whatever reasons, but the cry and suffering of that woman are heard by God, and He will arrange all things together for everything to be in the perfect alignment to lift her up, and her loved ones to do the same. Only on this planet Earth is where we know that time exists. That is why we feel that years pass by, and we do not see anything clearly. But, do you remember that for God a year is like a day and a day like a year? Well, let us be anxious for nothing. Relax; let us enjoy every second of our existence. Life was so beautifully instituted and set before us to have fun and enjoy everything that was created just thinking of us. We all have shattered dreams, because what we create with this finite mind of ours is not perfect. That is the reason for our struggles and stumbling. That is a way of God telling us that we are going in the wrong direction. By us gathering the leftover pieces of our shattered dreams and getting ready to create something new with them, it is a way of God directing our steps towards the right and truthful path. There are some of us that feel that our whole world crumbles, and we may even think of taking our own life away. The pain of the loss is so devastating, that we do not have the strength to even open our eyes, much less to think of getting up. It is okay, we need time to re-adjust and conform. God, in his infinite love, knows what we need to rise up to continue the path assigned for us on this wide earth. Since He made us, maybe he will reveal Himself to us in a dream, a vision, or He may even talk to us through a loved one, a friend, or a complete stranger, who will open up our understanding for us to know the right way, make the decision and then act upon it. Remember that we are not alone. There are the good and the bad among us. So, we must get all our strength to fight the battle we are confronted with each and every day. We must never forget: we are winners, Jesus paid it all at the cross. There are more for us than those against us. But, yes, there are those against us that, with the huge noise they use to scare us, we think that they are really more than the ones that are for us, but it is a lie. So, it is okay to be afraid sometimes, but for a short while. Let us go back to the truth, and remember that we are more than conquerors and winners. If God is for us, who can be against us? No one! A stumble or two does not make us losers, but wiser and smarter to fight the next battle and all the required battles we have to engage in to defend our mission and the ones assigned to our care. We can never give up. Remember that there are millions upon millions of witnesses in the heavenly places watching our response to the enemy's attacks. But of course, we cannot just be fighting randomly, not knowing the purpose of what we are doing. We must have a plan of action and foresee the result before we enter into the battle. That is why, if we do not have the direction from God, let us not move. The direction will come, but we just have to stay still. Let us not be deceived. The enemy masquerades himself as God, but do not forget to check the fruits. By the fruits of that person or persons, we will determine if they are for us or against us. Let us run as fast as we can from the enemy. Because, if we stay longer than we have to, the enemy may confuse us more, and entangle us in that situation for more time than is needed. This will weaken and confuse us, so that we may lose the next battle, and maybe even the next one, but remember; it does not matter how the situation is set up in front of us, know that the war has been won. Sooner or later we will know the truth, and the truth will set us FREE!

Shattered dreams? There are times in our lives when the shattering of our dreams is very deep and irreparable. However, we do not want to give up our hopes and expectations of that what was once precious to us. We try and try to mend the pieces, because we want to see those dreams come true one way or the other. We worked so hard, we planned for so long, just to let go like that? No way, we say to ourselves. We fight the good fight. We get all the resources, the information, whatever it takes for us to not let go of that illusion that we created in our mind. Sometimes we almost felt it, it was so real, it was there, just a couple of days, or sometimes even hours, or minutes to have it, but... All of a sudden, it was gone. What happened? We start to let our imagination fly to find the reasons for this and that, so we can try to make some sense of our loss. We struggle to accept the shattering and brokenness of our dreams. It is human to resist the change, the starting all over again. We do not understand. Why? If everything was going so perfectly well, we had everything under control. Everything was so carefully planned. Why, Why? When we are exhausted from not finding the reason for our misfortune, as we call it, and after we do not have anyone or anything else to blame, then we start to punish ourselves. We did something wrong. What if we had just awakened few minutes earlier, we tried to get up, but we stopped the alarm and overslept for 5 more minutes, what if we had not taken that route, what if... All the blame is ours, because we do not accept the facts. We must make peace in our minds, which are screaming and demanding an explanation. We, in the meantime, are killing ourselves with that guilt and disappointment. Stop! Have you thought about the dream itself? Yes, that goal that you set, that dream that you created in your imagination. Think about it. Was that a thing, or was that a person that was going to honor you and be a blessing to your life and others'? You may keep saying: Yes, Yes. But, let us be realistic. Sometimes we live in a fantasy world among things and people that do not belong to us. We make it look so perfect, that we start believing it. The infinite mind of God knows the result tons of miles ahead of us. Therefore, anything or any person that might end up diminishing or harming us in any way, will disintegrate. But how can you say that? You may ask. Well, think for yourself and you will confirm this. For those of us that are going through the middle of the change, we do not understand it and cannot make anything out of the feeling of discomfort. We expected so much, and what was delivered was so little. Well, welcome to the real life experiences. Just think that there are times when whatever we constructed must be demolished to the ground. What? Yes. There are times when we have to go through the deficit and defeat to find the real other you that you did not even think existed. When time passes, and the wound of that demolishing process takes place and heals, it is then, and only then, that we realize that if we had to go through that valley of shadow of death all over again to obtain that beautiful thing or person in our life, that we had never even thought could exist for us; we would gladly do it! There are times when we build on top of the ashes of the previous dream before we even pick up the pieces; later we realize that we have to let go and start brand new in a different place. Sometimes whatever we have from the previous experience is poisonous, and it does not matter if we are building with pure gold. The fact that we have a poisonous piece to add to the dough at the time of mixing, it will spoil the whole batch. Let us think twice before we make a final judgment or decision with those pieces left from our shattered dreams. Sometimes it is better to forget about everything we had from the dream that we are trying to save and start fresh all over again, but with a brand new idea. Who knows, maybe this time the result could be much better than the previous one. Bottom line. It does not matter what we deal with in our life, there is always an answer or solution to our dilemma.

Shattered dreams? Many times, because it is not a matter of if, but of when. We have to be aware of the so-called "disillusions", better-called "shattered dreams", so we can be prepared to encounter them and get over the bumps in our life. There are many ways of getting to our destination, and we walk them all. Since our birth until our death, we go through the same paths in life. Some are exactly the same roads, but of course, some are a little bit different. The destination is the same: birth, marriage, parenthood, empty nest, golden years, and death. What makes the difference a little bit on the different paths is what goes on between one station to the other, but the situations are the same as described above. We all have the same roles one-way or the other. Yes, I understand that some of us may not get married, but again, we have those relatives that are close to us, who demand our time and effort in whatever way. Also, we may not experience parenthood, but we have those nephews and nieces, who require of our help or advice through their childhood, and some of them see us like their second parents. So, as you can see, we all go through the same roads and highways until our final destination. No wonder we were created equal. We all experience the same joyful and sad moments in life, so we can relate when others go through the same things. It does not matter how well-educated or illiterate we are, the pain or happiness our hearts feel is the same. Maybe we can relate to one group better than another at a specific time, but we are humans and care for each other. It does not matter what part of the world goes through war, when we see the suffering of other human beings like ourselves, we feel their sadness and pain, because we can relate when we see their struggles. This is the beauty of belonging to this vast and wide family, because that is what we are: the human race, one big family. The color of our skin, the language we speak, or the governments we have are not barriers to relate and connect in spirit. Even without words, when our eyes meet, we can feel the others' happiness or sadness. We, by nature are willing to help or applaud according to the situation. When someone looks at us and gives us one of the most beautiful gifts this life can offer; a smile, we automatically smile back by instinct. Why? Because God wired us and formed us with the same material, so we can feel and relate to each other. The elderly have experienced and lived more things than the youth. Thank God we have those who have walked the road ahead of us, so they can tell us what to expect on that path new to the inexperienced. There is nothing to be afraid of, because there are many of us who have walked the road first, and are witnesses to those experiences, and are still alive; we did not die at the crossing. Our elders have experienced the same as some of us are experiencing now, and some little ones may experience tomorrow. Since the creation of man, the same path of life has always existed and will always exist until the end of our era on this earth. Therefore, the enjoyment and fulfillment of each moment is the most important thing for each one of us to never forget. It is so sad that some of us forget to live in the present and are so stuck in the experiences of the past, that we cannot look forward to a brighter and better future. If we cannot look forward to the future, how can we enjoy the present? Life is a living hell for those who are lost in the past and who do not want help to overcome that experience which has them stuck in the past. If we were the only ones harmed by our decisions, that would be perfectly fine, except that we are bringing innocent people down with us. When we have a downfall of any kind, and we have to make a choice, let us not rush to make a drastic decision without thinking it over, and meditating on the consequences of our actions when it comes to affecting others. Life is precious and it is too short, we cannot just waste it on worthless things. For sure, we can be better educated and ready to stand still when we have to fight with all our might to conquer the battle. Remember, we may lose the combat, but what matters is winning the war! This is the purpose of our sharing: to encourage you to never give up, but to arise and continue the fight. Nothing is over until it is really over. Changes and challenges are part of life. It is up to us to be prepared to confront them in a more relaxed and smooth manner.

The beauty of all the experiences in the end is that after picking up all the pieces from the different shattered dreams, we get wiser, and one day, all of a sudden, we can tell the difference between a rewarding and a one-way relationship. This last one is only looking for you when there is a need on someone else's part. This could be advice, or a listening ear. You may think, but what is wrong with that? Nothing, except that now you know when the person looking for you is just using you, like you have been used in the past. At that time you did not know that because you were always available for whoever needed you; you could not tell the difference. Now, when you have been in need, you really experienced the contrast. There have been those instances when you called that same person, just to talk, but there was no time for you. Usually, self-centered people do not consider others. Now you know. You are wiser and can differentiate who is who. That is a big plus in your agenda.

Nothing is forever. No matter how difficult and harsh the circumstances may be, sooner or later we will get over them. The same goes for human beings. Some are part of our lives forever until death sets us apart, and some are just for months or days, and some just cross our paths once, but that once; they may mark us forever. Ask the family of the girl who was happily running around the park. She just wanted to lose a couple of pounds to fit into that beautiful dress that was awaiting in her bedroom for the anxious and most important day of her life; her wedding day that was going to be within a week. Well, that one encounter with this person changed the role of her life. Her dreams were shattered, in fact, they were broken with no way to mend or put back together again. She was raped and killed. This one encounter destroyed not only this poor girl, but can you imagine all the people involved and devastated by this egocentric individual? The groom's dreams were shattered, as were the parents', the relatives' and friends'. One simple mistake on one's part, spun out of control, and many lives were destroyed. As you can see, you are not the only one whose dreams have been shattered and broken. There are many other lives, whose testimonies compared with ours, are nightmares of the worse category that one can ever imagine.

What about that couple who brought their teenagers to the movies? The father started the conversation while waiting in line to pay for the tickets. That one conversation made space for the second and the third conversation that ended being a relationship for days, until the wife of the new acquaintance was introduced to the family; these lives were changed forever. This woman was tired of her own husband, who was a loser, according to her, so she was on the search for someone "rich" who could give her everything her own husband could not provide. When she met this family, she was attracted to the husband. She became a really close friend to the wife, to the point that she basically became part of that family. The only time she was not there was when she went back to her house to sleep, otherwise she would be this family all the time. For some reason, when people have not experienced adversity in their lives or their closed ones, they are naive to danger, or maybe because they believe that everyone is like themselves, always wanting the best for others as for themselves. The point is that this malicious woman was obsessed in having this family and way of life for herself, that one day she planned a way to accomplish her evil goal. She cut the brake fluid hose of her friend's car, and when the mother of these five kids was driving down a hill, she lost control of the car and had a head-on collision. The driver of the other car, a teenager, son of another family, who was their only child, was killed on impact. The wife made it to the hospital. Her family was able to see her and be with her at the hospital, but they were not able to communicate with her ever again, because she was in comma until she died a couple of days later. This recently new woman in the life of this family, found the way to get close to the widower and father of five, 17, 15, 13, 11 and 9 year old; all boys. This woman was so evil, or should I say, mentally sick? She also planned the death of her own husband, who was insulin dependent. Because he was suffering from diabetes for decades now, no one questioned when the poor man died. The woman knows what she did, but she reported that her husband suffered a diabetic attack and she could not help him. Really? It is possible, but right after her husband's burial, she moved to live with the widower and the five boys, who had just received the mother's life insurance police of $500,000. But, thank God that He is just. This evil woman's plan did not prevail, because she had nightmares, and one night in her sleep she talked about being chased by the police and found guilty in court. She was screaming because she did not want to go to jail. Of course, the widower was awake and started asking her questions while she was in her dream. Guess what? Yes, she honestly answered to each question, and this was the way the poor man discovered that this woman was after his money and the commodity he could offer her, and that she planned his wife's death and her husband's.

Do you see how one person can disturb the lives of so many people? This woman without thinking it thoroughly, shattered so many people's dreams: The teenager, who lost his life in the car accident, did not even meet this woman, but her ambition and evil thoughts affected him, his parents and all his family. So, we can also say that sometimes we are victims of strangers' wrong doings. What can I tell you about these lives' shattered dreams? If we went through the ramifications of this one woman's plans and wickedness, we could write books and books. It was not only her life destroyed, because she ended up in jail, but can you imagine all the innocent people touched by the consequences of one act?

There are other encounters that last longer than days or months. For instance, these three attorneys met in their youth when they were in high school. They kept going to the same school. In fact, when deciding what career to embark on, the three of them agreed that they were going to be the best attorneys in the country, they were going to work together in a law firm of their own. Each of them was going to specialize in a different kind of law, but with the same purpose; to serve the people in need. Their service was going to be provided at no charge at front, but they were going to be paid from the settlement amount. However, there is always someone with that extra ambition that does not care or respect previous agreements. That is exactly what happened. One of the three partners, the youngest, thought that he was the smartest, and found a way to charge people at front, promising to get them their money back at the time of the settlement. But, of course, they were not going to disclose the agreement made at closed doors with him. It is obvious that dishonest people find their way to meet with their kind. This kept going until there was a law suit from one of the clients, who was not happy and knew that there was a loose string that he could pull any time that he found appropriate, and he did. When the firm had to defend itself in court, the other two partners were surprised to learn all the things this deceitful partner was capable of doing, and put all of them in such a predicament. The law firm lost the law suit and you can imagine the rest. All of them had to pay, and lost in the process of leveling the boat after the turmoil left from that bad decision this one person made.

We could keep going on and on with the different situations that we know along the way on our journey through this life. However, it does not matter how we explain it, the common denominator is the same; selfishness, which is the core of all evil and harm to others. Well, it is impossible to put it that simple. It does not matter if just an individual is physically or emotionally harmed, at the end, others are also touched by the result of the bad intentions of that one individual. If it is the wife who will be affected if the husband is harmed somehow, just think: The people the husband harmed pushed him off the road. Well, the husband is all in bruises and cannot move. Guess who will take care of him? Of course, the wife, who had her routine of doing things, but now, she has to wake up in the middle of the night, the husband is in pain and she needs to give him his medicine, etc. It does not matter how small or how big the consequences of one's wrongdoings are; those affect other people.

We have to be considerate to others and ourselves. Our world was created, and it is meant to be perfect. Even though the sunrises and sunsets are unique and different every single day, the sun complies with its duty to life on the earth. We can say the same thing about the moon and the stars that mark the seasons within the year. The trees, the plants, and every single creature on the planet earth. But what about us, the human beings, who are called to be in control and subdue everything that exists under the sun? We are the purpose of everything around us, which was created for our enjoyment and for our benefit.

It is so sad to see that we take all the beauty around us for granted. We do not appreciate the greatness of the sea. We see the big ships and machinery on the ocean spilling oil, to say the least of what really happens in our waters, causing the death of thousands of animals. The same thing happens with the animals in the jungle; some of the species are in extinction. Our polluted air is the result of all the ambitious plans of men, that demand the cutting of trees and the using of the land to build those big cities, roads and refineries. All these are meant for good of humanity, but we have gone to the extremes to import and export our merchandise to other countries. Yes, we are sophisticated and more advanced in our technology. What is wrong with showing our discoveries and expanding our businesses? Nothing. The result we all can see is that we are sacrificing other innocent creatures, and at the end, ourselves. The consequence of our greediness is our fast approach to our own destruction. The hard work of humanitarian groups trying to prevent the disastrous end is in vain if we do not cooperate with the cause of respecting us among each other first, then our community, our country, and the beautiful world we share and live in. The purpose of these stories is to awaken our senses, and to realize that all the suffering we see around the world is the result of someone's mistake or wrongdoing. An individual's idea that shattered someone else's dream, and that someone's hurt and pain touched someone else's life, causing the same effect; an unstoppable and contagious virus that has seduced and brought our society and our world to the state we are in. Some of us are co-dependent on drugs, alcohol, pornography, prostitution and despair all over the world. We must stop! We can start making the difference. We can try to reverse the effects of our own wrongdoings. Yes, our wrongdoings. It does not matter how many generations back the wickedness started, and you may think that you have not done anything wrong. Remember that we are all related in one-way or another. We are connected in a unique and special oneness. Therefore, if you and I start to break the effect, the movement towards the right direction is going to create an impact that the rest are going to feel and see. It doesn't matter how small the effect we create is, our close ones are going to react in a positive way towards it, and if we impact our household first, then our relatives and friends, and they do the same; one day we can touch our governments and the rest of the world. Let us never let the light in us be extinguished by the shattering of our dreams, but fortify it by focusing our eyes in the end result of our mission on this earth. Remember. We are here just for a little while:

19_____ to _____.

That is what will be read on our gravestone. Therefore, let us all fight the good fight, never giving up, but keeping our heads up with the conviction that we are warriors and conquerors in JESUS CHRIST, The Amen!

Our Shattered Dreams

Yesterday is gone, tomorrow may not come, but today is what counts!

- It is never too late to start.

- Every breath of life is an opportunity.

- It is okay to be you, just the way you are.

- No one else is like you. You are unique.

- Every challenge is a victory.

- Your calling and purpose are only for you.

What will be written on your gravestone and gospel of your name?

_____ To _____

Printed in the United States
By Bookmasters

Printed in the United States
By Bookmasters